TRUE BLUE

Davie Cooper of Glasgow Rangers has been described as the most naturally gifted player in British football since George Best. It is a reasonable and fitting tribute to a footballing genius who has been Scotland's most entertaining player for the past decade. In that time, the once unpredictable Clydebank player has turned into an international star.

TRUE BLUE is the autobiography that fans — and the press — have been waiting for: the remarkable tale of a gifted footballer who, for once, hasn't simply let his feet do the talking. Cooper gives us a unique insight into the world of a complete professional football player . . . a world that includes all the big names, the club he loves, the country he proudly represents. He has played alongside all the great names in Scotland's past and present, from Dalglish to Nicholas. Now he is in the middle of the Ibrox revolution inspired by such as Graeme Souness and Terry Butcher. And he has served under some of the most outstanding and controversial managers of our time . . . Jock Stein, Jock Wallace, Ally MacLeod, John Greig, Alex Ferguson and Andy Roxburgh, to name but a few. *TRUE BLUE* tells his own side of the story for the first time.

RANGERS LEGENDS

DAVIE COOPER

DAVIE COOPER with GRAHAM CLARK

MAINSTREAM
PUBLISHING

EDINBURGH AND LONDON

This edition produced exclusively for
Rangers Football Club

First published in Great Britain in 1987 by
MAINSTREAM PUBLISHING COMPANY (EDINBURGH) LTD
7 Albany Street
Edinburgh EH1 3UG

This edition produced exclusively for Rangers Football Club 2001

ISBN 1 84018 540 6

A catalogue record for this book is available from the British Library

Printed and bound in Great Britain by
Cox and Wyman Ltd

Contents

Foreword
by
Graeme Souness

THIS is the ideal opportunity for me to say exactly what I think about Davie Cooper, or, as he's better known at Ibrox, Albert. The nickname stems from *Coronation Street*'s Albert Tatlock who was always moaning and, believe me, that's what Coop does constantly. I can tell if he's going to have a good game when he reports and starts moaning. It's an encouraging sign.

More seriously, though, any manager would be delighted to have a player of his ability, talent and skill in the team. Basically, I believe he is more naturally gifted than Kenny Dalglish. And I'm delighted to say that from all accounts he has played better in recent times than he has done at any other stage of his career. He has been a revelation and as far as I can tell the reason for his more consistent approach is simply that he is surrounded by better players. Lads like Terry Butcher, Chris Woods and Graham Roberts are top-class professionals and Davie has responded accordingly.

From being a big fish in a small pool he is now just one of many outstanding players and it has taken a lot of pressure off him. He is enjoying his football as a result and that is reflected in his performances which have been outstanding for me. Now he is hungry for success and our domestic triumphs in the Premier League and the Skol Cup last season have whetted his appetite for more.

I see no reason why he cannot continue to be a huge asset, a match-winner in his own right, for Rangers Football Club for several more seasons. And if that proves to be the case, as I expect it to, no one will be more delighted than me.

Ibrox Stadium,
Glasgow.
August 1987.

Chapter One

MOODY BLUE

MOODY BLUE. That's the nickname I was given years ago when I was younger and it does have a kind of ring to it, doesn't it? Certainly, it appealed to Scotland's football writers who latched on to it at every available opportunity until Davie Cooper and Moody Blue were synonymous. Yet it had all started off simply because I was too nervous to talk to the media.

I was at Kilbowie at the time and ironically it was when we were in the middle of a great series of Scottish Cup games against Rangers that Clydebank and one Davie Cooper Esq. were pushed firmly into the public eye. Newspapers, radio stations and television crews all wanted to talk to me because I had done quite well against the Ibrox side but the truth of the matter is that I was just too uptight about talking in public to go and have a word with any of them. I was very quiet generally and the last thing I needed was to make a fool of myself in front of a microphone.

The attention then, though, was just a temporary thing and it wasn't until I joined Rangers that I was more and more in the spotlight. For a while at Ibrox I felt reporters were a bit unkind in the things they said about me so I simply decided one day not to speak to any of them. It was quite a deliberate decision because I thought I had been taking some stick I didn't deserve and reckoned they would write things anyway, so why should I help? Equally I

9

decided there could be no exceptions although I always tried to be very polite about it. I refused all interviews in the nicest possible way and gradually the Moody Blue thing snowballed.

It was never a problem to me personally although I think the family became a bit fed up with it all. Reporters are very persistent people and if I wasn't at home or if I was unavailable it fell to my folks or my wife Christine to take all the calls. Sports writers tried and failed, so papers sent feature writers who met with the same fate. Then it would be newsmen — or women — and I strategically avoided them too.

Looking back on it now it was, I suppose, all a bit silly, especially since I discovered to my advantage that they were really all on my side generally anyway. That came to light around May 1985, when my contract with Rangers was rapidly running out and I wasn't really looking like making much headway with a new agreement. The Press pitched in with their thoughts and it was clear the majority all felt the club should, basically, see me alright, even if that meant breaking all existing and traditional values placed on players.

When I realised that the media — always a powerful force — were batting for me I reasoned that they weren't so bad after all and ever since then we have enjoyed a good relationship. In retrospect, though, I think I would always have preferred "The Quiet Man" to "Moody Blue" because I have always been a bit reserved, although I hope never rude.

That characteristic goes back a long, long way. All the way, if you like to 25 February 1956 when little Davie arrived on the scene courtesy of Jean and John Cooper. I was my parents' second child. They had had John Junior three years previously but it didn't take long for them to realise he and I were complete opposites. John was a right little tearaway who was always getting into mischief whereas I would never do a thing wrong. Honestly! As I grew older I would hardly go out of the house to play and I have to admit I was more or less a mummy's boy.

At that time the family was in a flat at 4 Barrack Street in Hamilton and dad was working at the Lanarkshire Steel Works in nearby Motherwell. Mum, too, worked after I was old enough to go to the local Beckford Street Primary School which John attended as well. Around then we moved to another flat at 25 Brankholm Brae in Hillhouse which is also in Hamilton and where the family stayed for 20-odd years. That meant a change of school to Udston Primary but there was no change in me. I was still quiet,

10

Having a ball . . . and I'm only 18 months old.

content to mess about in the house playing with my toy cars and, basically, doing no harm to anyone.

But then John stepped in when I was nine and obviously decided to get me out and about and get me involved in football which had never held any interest whatsoever. John, in fact, had to drag me out of the house to play and he would stick me between the posts — or more often than not between the jackets — when he and his pals were a man short. I never kidded myself that they wanted me for my ability. They simply wanted a body and mine was the nearest and most available so I became an instant goalkeeper.

Chris Woods, Jim Leighton and Co. were never under any threat, mind you, because just as soon as I was allowed to make up my own mind I was playing outfield. Not for me that daft diving about on the ash pitches or the mud. Instead I moved to left-half for my school team. Actually it was left-half in the first half and inside-left in the second half! I was also captain which at the time was a great honour.

By then, strangely in view of my previous reluctance to get involved, I couldn't get enough football. It was like a drug. I was playing every minute I could and very little interrupted me and my football. One thing that did was mum pulling me indoors to have my tea and then warning me not to rush it in case I got indigestion. I always rushed it and, needless to say, I always got indigestion. The other interruption was nightfall. How I hated the darkness. I know it's inevitable but you try telling a nine-year-old fitba'-daft boy that.

Thankfully my school football wasn't affected by that problem and we had a great team at Udston. One season we went all the way unbeaten and picked up the Shinwell Cup after we beat Low Waters Primary 4-2 in the final at Hamilton Accies' Douglas Park. I scored a goal in that match and I remember Billy Holmes, brother of Morton's Jim, was in the opposition ranks that day.

We won the League shield as well and there was another tournament we would have won too but the organisers wouldn't let us into it. They said, as I recall, that our entry form arrived too late — but we all knew they wanted to give another team a chance! I don't really know why we were so good although we did have a couple of big lads playing for us and at that level that always helps. One, a boy called Billy Paterson, was huge and I seem to remember he caused opponents a fair bit of bother.

On the very rare occasions I wasn't playing I really enjoyed going to watch . . . Rangers. They were the only team I went to see

What a team . . . and me Captain of Udston Primary into the bargain.

and dad and I would walk down to Burnbank to get a lift to Ibrox with a man called — would you believe — John Stein. I also used to get on The Lariat Rangers Supporters Club bus which left from the pub where my mum sometimes worked, so altogether I managed to get to quite a few games.

Unlike other youngsters I had no particular heroes, no one I would watch and say: That's how I would like to play. I suppose the nearest I had to that was former Rangers and Scotland star Willie Johnston but I never consciously modelled myself on him. Basically I was too busy doing my own thing and one or two people who had watched me were equally busy telling dad that if I didn't make it in the game then they didn't know their football. And I was only 10 or 11 by then.

Time, indeed, to move on to St John's Grammar. Not to put too fine a point on it, I hated school. I think that might have something to do with the fact that St John's was a disaster football-wise. Nobody seemed to bother and I don't think there was an organised team until you got to about the third year. That was no use to me but happily Bill and Rose McKenzie came to my rescue. They decided to start up a team called Udston United and it's not too melodramatic to say that if they hadn't I don't think I would have continued playing. There was no other team I fancied and I'm sure I would have drifted away from football into something else.

Bill used to sit me in his car and together we would go round the houses knocking on doors, arranging for players to turn up on the Saturday morning. He would also organise raffles and the like to raise funds and I with one or two of the other lads would get the job of selling the tickets.

Saturday mornings were all I lived for and by now the game was an obsession. I would play in all weathers, in all conditions, and if I wasn't playing for Udston I would be banging a ball about. By myself if necessary. Football was my only thought. All of which didn't exactly help my academic career but I reckon I was always a lost cause in that direction. I'm not particularly proud of that but I couldn't help it. I was interested only in football.

The one other sport I did mess about with at that time — very briefly — was tennis but I was as impatient then as I am now and I didn't fancy always having to queue up to use the local courts. As it happens, I love the game now but then it was football, football and more football.

It was the same story for brother John too and I watched with great interest when he went south to Hull City when he was just 16. He was a winger and plenty of people would tell you he was a better player than I. John's problem was that he wasn't dedicated enough. He liked a good time. But he hated Hull and after a couple of years returned to Scotland. He had been staying in digs and got very homesick so he came back north and played regularly for Hamilton before going junior with Larkhall Thistle. I think his experience put me off going to England because although I had plenty of chances later on I always thought of how if John couldn't stick it because he wanted home, what hope would I have.

By now I was playing for Hamilton Avondale, a local team run by brothers Stuart and Alan Noble and they were to be my next mentors. I was in their Under-16 side and then their Under-18 team and in both cases I was one of the youngest players. I suppose that says something for my ability at the time. Someone must have thought I had a bit of talent anyway for I was soon picking up my first representative honours for Scotland. I was chosen for the Scottish Amateur League side and the Youth (Under-18) team.

They were great days and the League side won the Black Trophy by beating Ayrshire 1-0. I also played all three home internationals against England, Northern Ireland and Wales for the Youth side. One other familiar name at that time in those teams was Sharp but it wasn't Graeme who has gone on to play for Everton and Scotland but his brother Richard who I think is in the police nowadays. But playing for these representative sides certainly caused a bit of a stir, for it was then that senior clubs began to take an interest in me.

Stuart and Alan had given me a job as an apprentice printer in their works in Almada Street in Hamilton and I was quite happy learning a trade and playing for Avondale, even if there appeared to be plenty of other people who thought I would be happier just playing football. Clubs came on the scene from what seemed like all corners of the country and they watched me play regularly for Avondale and in the representative games.

One game we played in Ashgill and there were a few scouts there. It was Grand National Day and we were winning easily. I remember taking time out to find out from dad and John, who were watching, exactly how the big race had gone. Then, as now, I liked a flutter on the horses. But even that slight wavering of concentration didn't seem to put the scouts off because they continued to call Stuart, Alan and dad at regular intervals.

Coventry City were the first English club to show an interest and they were certainly professional about it. They sent me up a glossy brochure outlining the training facilities, the digs and anything else that they thought might attract someone to Highfield Road. Crystal Palace were there as well and one or two others into the bargain. But I always thought back to John and his trials and tribulations down south and I never encouraged them.

As it was, there was plenty of Scottish interest as well and I had a trial with Clyde when I scored a goal in a reserve match. Then Shawfield manager Stan Anderson immediately offered me £4 a week, but while I was flattered I didn't exactly beat a return path to his door.

Motherwell, managed by Ian St John, were also quite enthusiastic about signing me and the Saint made me an offer. He reckoned that I could be farmed out to a junior side because I needed building up. Building up? I had watched John play junior football and if that was what was needed to build me up then it was thanks but no thanks. John used to get kicked up and down the park and that wasn't for me.

Clydebank were right in there and they made me a more inviting offer that didn't involve junior football, though the travelling put me off. I know Clydebank isn't far but, remember, I was working in Hamilton and it would have caused a few problems.

So it went on and most clubs were credited with having an interest of some sort. That included Rangers but I looked at them and thought they had so many players I would never get a game. That was the first time I turned down the Ibrox club. To be honest, it wasn't all that difficult a decision for the reason I have already explained. I know that might sound unbelievable to the thousands of youngsters around the world who would like nothing better than to play for Rangers but I felt it made sense at the time.

Even now, looking back on it, I feel I made a good decision, although with the benefit of hindsight I have been lucky the way things have turned out. I wasn't to know then that I would end up at Ibrox eventually so I suppose it was a massive gamble. But, like I say, I don't mind a gamble now and again.

Through all these offers and invitations I was lucky to have the family right behind me and, for that matter, people like Stuart and Alan and Bill and Rose. I could, and did, talk to them at various times and listened to what everyone had to say. They were good with advice but all stressed that the final decision was my own. In the end I decided against all the clubs who came in for me and stuck to what I was doing . . . working in the printer's and playing for Avondale.

The only drawback about that was that I grew old or at least too old for Avondale and being a bit fussy about who I played for I found myself not playing at all. My problem was, and still is, that I am essentially very family orientated and don't like to stray too far from my domestic scene. Heavens, when I was 12 and the parents of my pal Ronnie Nisbet asked me if I would like to go on holiday with them to Rimini I was delighted to accept. I went, really quite enjoyed it, but couldn't wait to get back to my pet half-collie Scot. I really missed that dog even though I was involved in my first trip outside of Britain.

That shows how home-loving I was and I found it very difficult to get a team that I thought I would enjoy and, more importantly, was local. So, at 18 years old, I chucked football. I packed it in without so much as a second thought and I know now that Stuart and Alan nearly had apoplexy. Obviously, they felt I was getting ready to throw reasonable talent down the drain and they weren't impressed. So unimpressed were they, in fact, that they actually contacted a club on my behalf even if I didn't know about it at the time!

They knew me better than most because I was still working for them. I had "graduated" from being an apprentice and all that entails, such as making the tea and sorting out the big fire that kept everyone warm in their works. Now I was actually making tickets and pamphlets and really quite enjoying it all. But, and I'll always be grateful to them for it, they believed I was destined for greater things. So while I was grafting away in their Almada Street works they were sorting out my future by putting in a call to Clydebank and, more specifically, Jack Steedman.

Now Jack, as I was to discover, is a very persuasive man who won't take no for an answer when he wants something. After all, I had already tried a "no" once but with Stuart and Alan's encouragement he came back to try again, even though I wasn't actively involved with football at all at the time.

Nothing daunted, Jack appeared outside work one day and when Stuart told me he was there I thought I should at least do him the courtesy of speaking about it, even if the prospect didn't exactly have me bubbling over. So out I went to sit in Jack's car — a big Jaguar — and I was quite impressed. Jack being Jack, he didn't mess about and he laid it on the line for me.

I can't begin to imagine what was running through his head when he was talking to me because even then I was showing a marked lack of enthusiasm for the whole prospect. The thought of continuing my job and then having to make my way to Clydebank for night-time training just didn't appeal and the fact that I didn't drive merely complicated the issue still further. That, to me, was the chief stumbling block to any deal that might take me to Kilbowie but Jack continued his sales pitch as if nothing was going wrong.

When you're faced with that kind of enthusiasm it's difficult not to feel wanted and deep down I knew I was desperately keen to start playing football again somewhere. It would be unfair of me to suggest that Jack then pulled his master-stroke by revealing an envelope with what looked to me like a king's ransom . . . but it certainly helped. Inside the envelope was £300 in grubby, used notes which he offered me as a signing-on fee. That, plus the promise of a decent basic wage plus more when I proved myself and worked my way into the first team, left me thinking that maybe it would all be worth it after all.

But I can honestly say that while the money was interesting to a youngster picking up a few quid in a printer's it didn't prove the be-all and end-all. That was simply Jack himself. He is such a likeable man and talks such a good game that I would have signed for him anyway. Mind you, if he reads this he'll probably want that £300 back!

So after half an hour in Jack Steedman's car my world was taking on a whole new look, even if I didn't really know quite what it had in store. Here was me a Clydebank player, and yet Jack's parting words weren't quite what I expected. "I'll see you in five or six weeks. You'll get a letter telling you when we expect you in for training," he said.

In all the excitement I had forgotten it was the middle of the summer and that Bankies, in common with all the other clubs, were finished with the season. It meant a few impatient weeks for me before I could go to Kilbowie and call myself a professional footballer.

Chapter Two

A STEPPING STONE TO GLORY

I was nothing if not confident when I made my way to training with Clydebank for the first time because when I looked at their squad I realised there were a few players who were on their way out and that in turn would leave openings for the likes of myself.

I wasn't being big-headed, just practical. I certainly didn't doubt my own ability and although I recognised I would have to feel my way a bit I didn't plan on being kept out of the first team for too long. Happily, I was proved right and although I started off in the reserves I was soon getting a call-up to bigger and better things.

I had worked hard at training — something I didn't enjoy then and still don't for that matter — and when I glanced around I saw the faces that were coming to the end of their careers. One, believe it or not, was Andy Roxburgh but I don't think either of us thought for a second at that time how we would end up over a decade later. Others around at the time included current Bankies' boss Sam Henderson and former coach Jim Fallon, Gregor Abel, Peter Kane and the inimitable Jim Gallacher who is still going strong in goals at Kilbowie.

They were a good group of lads working under coach Bill Munro — then as now there was no manager — and I thoroughly enjoyed myself most of the time. I say most of the time simply because just getting to Clydebank was, as I had suspected, a bit of a nightmare.

I was still working for the Nobles in Hamilton so when I left there I had to get a train to Glasgow where I picked up a bag of chips — the ideal meal before a training session! — then ran round to Queen Street Station where I caught another train that got me into Singer Station about ten minutes before we were due to start.

It wasn't really ideal and quite honestly I hated the routine. All that to get to something I didn't even like!

But training is a necessary evil and all we did for a while was run round and round the Kilbowie track. That was bad enough but those of you who know the ground will realise you had to pass the Social Club en route and every lap you would look up and see guys inside sipping their pints. I think that must be the definition of frustration.

But it was all worth it in the end because as I had anticipated I didn't have to wait too long for a first-team chance. That duly came and if my debut wasn't exactly memorable there were some marvellous moments in that first season.

We did quite well in the Scottish Cup for instance, and my first big game was against Dunfermline in that tournament. We won 2-1 and a First Division scalp was under the belt of the little Second Division side. More importantly, though, was what was in store for the winners of that game — a fourth-round tie against Celtic. Jock Stein, then manager of the Parkhead side, had watched the match and we must have given him some food for thought.

So it was on to Parkhead and my first look at the ground. To be brutally frank I didn't think much of it then and I don't think much of it now. The pitch is one I have never felt comfortable playing on any time and that, plus my dislike of Celtic anyway, gave me a strange feeling. I was nervous for a start and that is not like me but it was a big occasion and I wasn't exactly used to them.

Celtic paraded all their stars including Kenny Dalglish, George Connelly, Harry Hood, Dixie Deans . . . and Danny McGrain. I was in direct opposition to Danny and I'm delighted to say I gave him a hard time that afternoon. As the game went on I grew more and more confident and as that happened Danny liked it less and less.

Not that it was a one-man show. Far from it. Bankies were doing so well we stunned Celtic with an opening goal through Joe McCallan midway through the first half. Unfortunately they fought back well and two goals from Dalglish plus one apiece from Jackie McNamara and Roddie McDonald put paid to our Cup efforts.

A Clydebank player . . . and proud of it.

But we hadn't been disgraced in any way and, on the contrary, we had put up a good show. That, plus the fact that I felt I had done really well against McGrain and that Jack Steedman was delighted with the club's share of the gate receipts, took the sting out of the defeat. It was, essentially, the first time I had been noticed by anyone outside of Clydebank. I only wish I had scored a goal that day because that would have given me an awful lot of pleasure. Still, overall it was a good season for me considering it was my first in the game and I enjoyed every minute of the involvement at Kilbowie.

The summer that followed was important because that's when I met Christine, who was later to become my wife. We met, ironically in view of the time of year, at a skating rink in Hamilton and then a few times thereafter at the club where I went to play darts with my brother John and our mates.

So life in general was good and in a football sense it was all set to get even better. By now I had arranged lifts to Kilbowie from team-mates like Sam Goodwin and John Gilmour and midway through the season I was one of a handful of players Clydebank made full-time. It was a terrific boost although even afterwards I still went to the Nobles' printing work and did a few stints for them.

It was a major step, though, for Bankies to pledge themselves to full-time football even if it was for only a few players. There was not a lot of money about and it was a major gamble for the Second Division club. But Jack Steedman is not daft. He obviously looked into the future and decided Bankies were going places.

Naturally, he was right. We had some tremendous matches throughout the year and I like to think I contributed my fair share. Certainly I scored more goals than at any other time in my career, including the odd hat-trick. I got three goals against Alloa, for instance, but at the same time I was taking my fair share of stick from the opposition. One newspaper actually had a writer counting the number of times I was fouled and Jack Steedman helped him out by telling him it was 36 times in three games. He reckoned I was the most-fouled player in British football. Mind you, he also thought I was the worst trainer in the world, so what does he know!

It was a good Second Division race for promotion with ourselves, Raith Rovers and Alloa leading the charge and it was no surprise when it went virtually all the way before we took one of the spots. We clinched it, after 50 years of waiting by the local fans, with a 2-0 victory over Forfar at Kilbowie. Nothing much

Here's the proof that Clydebank have enjoyed moments of glory.

happened in the first half of that historic game but I opened the scoring with a penalty just after half-time and then McCallan ended the waiting and worrying by adding a second near the end.

It was a memorable day for the club and it wasn't a bad night either as we celebrated the occasion in the statutory manner. We went on to win the Championship, in fact, and my own personal reward for a good season came when Scotland manager Willie Ormond selected me in a First and Second Division squad for a game against a Highland League side.

The match was at Elgin's Boroughbriggs and when the squad met up it was the first time I got to know goalkeeper Jim Stewart who was to become a team-mate, and indeed room-mate, at Ibrox. I was the only Second Division player on at the start but to give you an idea of the company I was keeping Stuart Kennedy, who became an Aberdeen star, and Gordon Smith, who also ended up at Rangers, were in the team as well. We won 3-0 and while it won't rank as one of the great games of our time it was a good night for me and my first taste of an international-type get-together.

Around the same time I was getting a few mentions in the transfer front and one concrete offer came from Aston Villa. It was a £65,000 bid and I suppose most youngsters would have jumped at the chance of joining an English First Division club. But I didn't and I don't think the decision went down too well with their manager Ron Saunders. He seemed to think an offer of three times what I was getting at Clydebank would be enough to tempt me, but there's more to life than money.

I was really happy at Kilbowie and they weren't in any rush to sell me, even though Jack Steedman appeared to have a queue of managers lining up outside the door looking for my signature. Jack, who I admit is prone to exaggeration at times, said there were 11 clubs wanting me. But England might as well have been Outer Mongolia as far as I was concerned. I simply wasn't interested.

At that time I said that Rangers were the only club capable of changing my mind and although I knew they had been watching me, I was only half-serious. I felt I still had a lot to prove and while I might have done the business in the Second Division there was a new challenge ahead in the First. Time was on my side.

Some people suggested it was simply a lack of ambition that stopped me from moving at that point but that's not the case. I was ambitious enough but I also knew better than anyone else that maybe I wasn't quite ready for the English First Division. I was scarcely ready for our own First Division but despite that things went well and we were ready to embark on a series of games that probably changed my life.

By the September of 1976 Bankies were sitting proudly at the top of the League when we were drawn to play Rangers in the quarter-finals of the League Cup. It was a two-leg tie and we all looked forward to another crack at the big boys. After all, we reasoned, we hadn't done too badly against Celtic in an earlier Scottish Cup clash and over two games . . .? Rangers, though, were an awe-inspiring prospect, for they had won the treble the previous year and under Jock Wallace were always a hard side for any class of opposition. So off we went into the lion's den and it didn't take me long to find out the hard facts of life at the top.

The first game was at Ibrox and two minutes into the match I learned the ground rules according to John Greig. The man who later became my gaffer took exactly 120 seconds to let me know he was around. He waded in with the kind of assault that Jack the Ripper would have been proud of and then, just to rub salt into my wounds, growled: "If I get another chance I'll break your leg."

There's no doubt about it, Greigy gave you that warm, it's nice-to-be-wanted feeling. Not that he was alone, for it seemed to me that he and big Tam Forsyth took it in turns to put me up in the air, wait for me to come down again and then repeat the process. But even that treatment couldn't prevent me enjoying the match and especially so when we went ahead through Mike Larnach. Derek Johnstone equalised but Billy McColl put us ahead again from the penalty spot and that was how things stood at the interval.

There's no doubt that Rangers were then given a quiet reminder of what was expected of them by Wallace, for after half-time they hit us twice through Alex MacDonald and Johnny Hamilton to go 3-2 up. It seemed to be the end but I scored late on to complete a great night for us little 'uns. It was a glorious result and left us confident about the return game.

Before that, however, I was named in the Scotland Under-21 squad for an international against Czechoslovakia in Pilsen and maybe the call-up and my performance against Rangers moved coach Bill Munro to liken me to George Best. "Cheeky but brilliant" was the description he attached to us both, but even being mentioned in the same breath as Best was enough for me. Maybe the beard we both sported fooled him too.

Whatever, it all prompted me to do quite well again against Rangers in the second game at a packed Kilbowie and I actually scored the equaliser after John Greig had put Rangers in front. We survived extra time as well and then went and lost the toss for the right to stage the third match.

There was a small matter of the Under-21 game to be fitted in as well and my first senior representative honour was a tremendous experience, even if Czechoslovakia didn't exactly fill me with envy for people who live in the Eastern Bloc countries. Scotland drew 0-0 and coach Andy Roxburgh was pleased with the result and the way it had been achieved. We played some good football but it's not difficult to see why when you look through that team of over a decade ago. This was the line-up: Bobby Clark (Aberdeen), George Burley (Ipswich Town), Pat Stanton (Celtic), Roy Aitken (Celtic), Arthur Albiston (Manchester United), John Wark (Ipswich Town), Davie Narey (Dundee United), Tommy Burns (Celtic), Davie Cooper (Clydebank), Davie McNiven (Leeds United) and Paul Sturrock (Dundee United).

One other interesting thing about that side is the fact that Aitken, Albiston, Narey, Burns and Sturrock — all youngsters at the time — stayed with their clubs and are still doing the business.

Me? I was getting plenty of attention and I suppose around now I began to realise it was inevitable I would leave Clydebank sooner rather than later. But I still wasn't in any rush. There was the not insignificant matter of that League Cup tie against Rangers still to be decided plus Bankies' bid for promotion to the Premier League.

First things first, and that meant a 0-0 draw in the third game of the saga against Rangers. The only memorable happening in an otherwise boring draw was a fine Jim Gallacher save from an Alex Miller penalty. Eventually something had to give and in the fourth match at neutral Firhill it was us. Derek Parlane opened the scoring and I levelled it but Bobby McKean hit the winner after 390 minutes of action.

Those games, I am convinced, had a lot to do with me eventually going to Ibrox. Rangers went on to be beaten badly by Aberdeen in the League Cup semis and it was after that that they stepped up their search for new blood and I became the prime target.

There was other business to attend to, mind you, and we secured a second successive promotion — St Mirren were champions — when we got the necessary point against Dundee at Dens Park. Their star that day, incidentally, was none other than Gordon Strachan, and Tommy Gemmell was also in the side.

It had been an action-packed season but it was nothing compared to what was about to happen to me. My life turned upside down in the space of just a few days and I didn't have to kick a ball in that time! It was a real case of good news and bad news that started off an incredible couple of weeks for me.

The good news was that I was chosen by Ally MacLeod in the senior Scotland squad for the Home Internationals and the fact-finding tour to South America that was to be preparation for the following year's World Cup in Argentina. It was the stuff dreams are made of but my day quickly turned into a nightmare that same evening.

I was at The Lariat pub in Hamilton along with dad, John, Bill and Rose McKenzie and Christine, and we were all celebrating my call-up to the full international squad when John was called to the 'phone. He came back to tell us that mum's friend Mrs Paterson had been knocked down by a car as the two of them were returning from a night's bingo in Burnbank. Naturally, we 'phoned Hairmyres Hospital to find out how she was and they told us it was a Mrs Cooper who had been involved in the accident.

We were devastated and as always happens the hospital wouldn't give out any information about how serious the matter was. So, without any further ado, we rushed from the pub to the hospital in what was without question the longest and quietest

Happy and glorious. Bankies celebrate after promotion and among the familiar faces is, front right, Andy Roxburgh.

journey of my life. All sorts of thoughts rushed through my head and I'm sure dad and John were the same but somehow no one would voice their worst fears.

It was almost a relief when we got there to find mum lying on a stretcher apologising for spoiling our night out! By then, though,

27

we were just delighted she was alive, although the injuries were serious enough for her to be in hospital for six months afterwards. It was a traumatic day and if you can pack every conceivable emotion into 24 hours I did it then.

Meanwhile speculation was raging about my future and although I didn't play in the Home Internationals I was looking forward to putting the Clydebank name on the world map by getting a game on the South American tour. What I didn't realise was that I would be on the trip as a Rangers player.

The move that finally dragged me away from Kilbowie went through relatively quickly and without fuss. Jack Steedman, who was actually on holiday on the south coast of England with his wife Margaret, conducted negotiations from afar with Willie Waddell. He has since told me that the Ibrox club at first offered £50,000 and even when they upped the bid to £100,000 Jack insisted they were getting the bargain of all time!

My own part in the proceedings wasn't quite so straightforward although there were no major problems. The first I knew of it all was when Jock Wallace telephoned me at home to say he wanted to come out and talk personal terms. Shortly after that he called back to say it would be better if I went into Ibrox, so I set off with dad and John in a Fiat 125 Super that Clydebank had given me to help with the visits to mum at Hairmyres. I still couldn't drive so it was a nice gesture from Jack, knowing as he did that John would be the one who would be ferrying us all about. When we got to Ibrox dad stayed in the car while John and I went up those famous stairs.

No other club in the world could have enticed me even that far but by then I had weighed everything up and decided I didn't want to take the chance of turning Rangers down for a second time. I might like a gamble but there are times when commonsense prevails and this was one of them. Deep down I realised this was my big chance and I wasn't in the mood to blow it.

You get a tremendous feeling of history and achievement when you are at Ibrox. The place has an aura about it that Parkhead, for instance, just can't match. It would be enough to make the most experienced professional stop and wonder, so imagine what it did for a 21-year-old totally unused to a situation like it. After all, it was a bit different from sitting in Jack Steedman's car looking at used notes and that, remember, was my only previous connection with transfer business.

It didn't help either when I walked into the manager's office and came face to face with three of the biggest names in Rangers' history. When I left John in the Blue Room I strolled in to be confronted by general manager Willie Waddell, manager Jock Wallace and assistant manager Willie Thornton. It was a formidable combination.

To be quite honest I felt a bit like a schoolboy up in front of the headmaster — only there were three of them. What I didn't feel like was a professional footballer who was in reasonable demand and who should have been holding all the aces in transfer talks. But I was hardly genned up on that kind of thing and the deal was concluded within an hour of me arriving at the ground. Initially, Rangers offered me a signing-on fee of £5,000 but looking back on it I think even Messrs Waddell, Wallace and Thornton were a bit embarrassed by that because it didn't take much negotiating from me to get that figure doubled. At that point I was led to believe that after tax I would end up with something like half and that didn't seem too bad. I went out to have a word with John but he was so keen that I should sign that he would have let me accept a tenner never mind £10,000!

The basic wage was around £150 and there were bonuses per point, which all helped. I don't suppose it was a fortune compared with clubs down south but I was happy enough because I knew long before I sat down with the Rangers management trio that I would be signing almost regardless of the financial arrangements. I was never going to be a problem but, in retrospect, I got stung a bit because at the end of the day the taxman took £6,500 of my share to leave me with just £3,500.

I learned my lesson from that and when the time came again just a couple of years ago I thought back to that moment and vowed I would do better for myself in a new contract. Then, however, I was just well pleased to put my name down on the appropriate bit of paper and after telephoning Jack on holiday I did just that. Maybe he was right, maybe Rangers did get a bargain.

It's customary in deals like that for the club you are leaving to also weigh in with a few quid but Bankies didn't do that. Instead, Jack told me to keep the car they had given me and I appreciated that.

After the signing there was the usual media scramble and during it big Jock Wallace said some very nice things about me. He stated that I was "the most exciting prospect in Scottish football with tremendous ability, great skill, flair and can get goals as well. Basically, Cooper has it in him to become a real personality player and I can't wait to see him in a Rangers jersey."

But Jock had to bide his time because I had the Scotland tour and the rest of the summer to go before I reported back to Ibrox.

In the midst of all the drama I did spare a thought for Clydebank because I was sorry in many ways to be leaving Kilbowie. I had three great years there. It was a huge wrench to leave the lads and whatever I have achieved in the game is essentially down to the early guidance I received.

Clydebank were good for me at that stage of my career and hopefully I was good for them. We won two promotions to take us straight from the Second Division to the Premier League and I would like to think I could claim a fair share of the credit. But it was time to move on and from my point of view it was all developing as I wanted it to.

Chapter Three

RULES, REGULATIONS, RIO AND RANGERS

THE first thing I did as a Rangers player was disobey the rules and regulations the Ibrox club have as a kind of code of conduct for the players. But that sounds worse than it actually was because before the ink was dry on my new contract I was flying off with Scotland on a fact-finding tour of South America and I was still sporting the moustache I had had for years. Rangers didn't approve of anyone having any facial hair — I think they would even have frowned on eyebrows if they could have! — but I reckoned that I would be safe from the wrath of Jock Wallace over in Chile, Argentina and Brazil. So the moustache stayed and certainly Scotland boss Ally MacLeod didn't seem at all concerned about it as the squad left Glasgow for the long haul to Santiago.

The trip included three games against the aforementioned countries and while results are always important it was specifically designed to allow the management and the players a taste of what would lie ahead in the following year's World Cup finals in Argentina if Scotland were to get there. It was useful forward-planning — not always the Scottish Football Association's strong point at the time — and from my own point of view a marvellous adventure.

It was a squad bristling with talent and players such as Kenny Dalglish, Danny McGrain, Martin Buchan, Bruce Rioch, Willie

Johnston and Lou Macari were team-mates. And it's just as well there were one or two in that lot who were more or less my size. For when we got to our hotel in Santiago I discovered my one and only suitcase was missing. I couldn't believe it. I had personally left it with the rest of the luggage by the side of the bus at the airport but obviously it had been stolen.

So there I was on my first senior trip with Scotland and all I had to wear were the clothes I stood up in. The thought ran through my head then that another of Jock Wallace's rules was for players to be smart at all times when representing the club. It's just as well he was 10,000 miles away because I was wearing a moustache he didn't like and a variety of clothes that made me look more like Worzel Gummidge than Beau Brummel.

The rest of the lads were great and helped me out with bits and pieces of their own gear but grateful as I was I have to admit Gordon McQueen's shirt was like a coat on me. In due course one of the officials with the squad took me down town to buy some clothes but Santiago wasn't Sauchiehall Street and if I said the choice of gear was limited I would be exaggerating. Still, it was very hot and fortunately I could get by with the bare essentials so to speak.

I was rooming with Kilmarnock's Jim Stewart and I was delighted about that because I had met him previously and we were good friends. But we both got into bother with Ally MacLeod almost before the tour began in earnest and it didn't exactly get my Scotland career off to a flying start. It was an incredibly silly thing but it's stuck in my mind to this day and it made me wonder about Ally.

We were due to report in the hotel reception at seven o'clock to go training one night and Jimmy and I stepped out of the lift into the foyer at 6.50 p.m. We knew we were early if anything but just as we got out of the lift we heard Ally demanding where Cooper and Stewart were. When he saw us he enquired after a fashion as to where we had been. Didn't we know the time? Weren't we aware that when everyone was ready we just left? Jimmy and I couldn't believe it. We had been told to meet up at seven o'clock. We were early. And here we were getting a telling-off. We weren't too impressed to be honest.

The rest of the time in Chile was fairly straightforward, though, and we did well in the game. In fact, we hammered the local international side 4-2. Macari got a double and Dalglish and Asa Hartford got one apiece while I watched the action from the bench.

32

Santiago definitely wasn't my favourite place, however, and apart from the result and the exit signs from the country the only thing I liked was the onyx souvenirs. I bought a couple of pieces for Christine.

So it was on to Argentina and everyone was a bit taken aback when we saw that the 'plane which was to transport us over the mountains to Buenos Aires was painted a strange shade of pink. No one thought any more about it until we landed at the other end and it was then that someone explained the colour showed up well against the mountain snow. There were so many crashes and a pink 'plane was easy to locate even if it was in bits. I'm only glad I didn't know the reason before we took off.

It became clear even at the airport that Argentina were treating the whole thing as a dress rehearsal for the forthcoming World Cup because security was unbelievable. There would have been no chance of losing my suitcase there.

The coach that took us to the hotel had a couple of motor-cycle police outriders for company and, believe me, they didn't mess about. Anyone who got in our way would have found it less painful jumping off the Forth Road Bridge. The guys on the bikes would go up alongside cars who were going too slowly — maybe they were only doing 70 mph through the city centre — and rather than mess about with a lecture they literally kicked the sides of the vehicles as they went along. It was incredible. The cops would simply plant a size ten into the side of any offending cars. We saw that happen a few times but after that we were belting through Buenos Aires so quickly I shut my eyes. That kind of "security" followed us throughout our stay there. Armed guards patrolled the hotel corridors 24 hours a day and we even got to the stage of exchanging badges for bullets!

Obviously, they were leaving nothing to chance as they prepared for the World Cup and their international team took the whole thing seriously as well. We knew roughly what to expect in the match because England had had problems earlier and Trevor Cherry had been ordered off in ridiculous circumstances. We weren't disappointed.

It was a very physical game from the word go. Actually dirty would be a better description. Willie Johnston was kicked from one end of the park to the other and he later coined the great phrase about his marker saying he was a Sumo wrestler in studs. It was a good description and "Bud" took some terrible stick. After he had been whacked for what seemed like the fiftieth time

33

MacLeod told me to go and warm up. I don't think Ally realised it was raining coins. It really was very hostile and I wasn't too upset when Willie picked himself up and carried on. He must have wished he hadn't bothered for eventually he was sent off and if ever anyone was innocent — and it wasn't always the case with Willie — this was one such time.

The game finished 1-1 and it was all very unsavoury. They had playing for them a guy called Killer and that somehow summed it up. The only good thing about Argentina's performance was the part played by Ossie Ardiles. It was the first time he was really noticed outside of his own country. But we weren't sorry to leave and the contrast between Argentina and our next port of call, Brazil, could hardly have been greater.

Rio de Janeiro was magnificent. We stayed at the Sheraton Hotel which had its very own section of the famous Copacabana Beach. Without question it's the best place I have ever been. Rio was sensational and even if I was hardly a world traveller at the time I didn't need any encouragement to take in the beauty of the city. Obviously there were other parts I didn't see that I'm sure were dreadful and poverty-stricken but for me it was breathtaking where we were.

And the match wasn't bad either though we were a bit patched up after Buenos Aires. Even then I couldn't get a game but the lads were in no way disgraced, losing 2-0 in the magnificent Maracana Stadium, through goals from Zico and Cerezo.

To be fair I hadn't gone to South America with any great expectations about playing. Obviously I would have liked to but for a lad fresh out of Clydebank I was happy enough just being there. Mind you, I actually paid for the privilege because there's no doubt I was out of pocket by the time we arrived back in Scotland in late June. My problem was simply that I had never been away from home that long before and with mum still in hospital I spent literally hours on the telephone to the house.

I also 'phoned Christine a few times and once when I tried to get her at our house dad said she was at a neighbour's just up the road. Before I could tell him it didn't matter he was away to get her, leaving me on the other end of the line listening only to the sound of my money disappearing! But overall it was a tremendous experience and it all left me looking forward to joining Rangers properly.

What I wasn't so keen on was the thought of pre-season training with Jock Wallace. I had heard about the Gullane sands the Big Man used for conditioning the Ibrox lads and considering I didn't

Welcome to Ibrox . . . Tom Forsyth and John Greig (M.B.E. no less!)
greet me as a Rangers player.

even enjoy running round a track it was a fearsome prospect. But
in fairness to Jock there's no doubt in my mind it worked. A
moustache-less Davie Cooper survived it and I am convinced it
benefited everyone later on in the season when fitness was so
important on the heavy pitches.

It certainly didn't have an instant effect, though, for after a brief
trip up north for a few pre-season games I lined up against
Aberdeen for my competitive debut for the club on the opening
day of the season — and we lost 3-1. Bobby Russell and Billy
Mackay also played their first games that day at Pittodrie and I
think we would all have preferred an easier opening match.

If we thought that was bad, worse was to come. Rangers signed
Gordon Smith from Kilmarnock after that initial defeat but that
wasn't the bad news. What was happened the next Saturday and
that was a 2-0 home defeat at the hands of Hibs.

It certainly wasn't the most auspicious of starts but we were
hardly prepared for the demonstration against the management
that followed the game. A group of supporters stayed behind to
yell abuse and it was all a bit unnerving after just 180 minutes of the
season.

But there were no signs of panic inside Ibrox and gradually we turned our form around. And as we did so I began to realise just what a difference a crowd behind you can make. I wasn't too used to big attendances at Kilbowie but it was different with Rangers and the support was worth a goal of a start to us. It is very intimidating for opponents to know that 99 per cent of the crowd are desperate to see them lose and at the same time it is a huge boost for us.

We began to play really well around the October of 1977 and the month started with a home game against my old club. It was a special occasion for me, although I was a bit upset when they took the lead through Gerry Colgan. But after half-time I scored a couple — one direct from a corner — and Gordon Smith weighed in with a double as well to give us a comfortable 4-1 victory.

There were a few memorable games around that time. We had a series of matches in the League and League Cup against Aberdeen. We gained a bit of revenge for our opening day defeat by beating them 3-1 at Ibrox while in the League Cup we produced a devastating performance when we won 6-1 in the first leg at home, with Smith getting a hat-trick. Everything fell into place that night and Derek Johnstone, Alex Miller with a penalty and Alex MacDonald scored the other goals. Duncan Davidson scored for the Dons. The second game was always a formality as a result and for the record we lost 3-1 but were never in any danger of going out.

Afterwards, big Jock took the squad to St Andrews to stay over and prepare for a return to League business against Hibs at Easter Road. It was a good break and although I don't play golf the rest of the lads did, in between training sessions.

Instead of golfing I lazed around the hotel and stuck a couple of bets on the horses. On the Friday afternoon I did what's called a roll-up and put money on four nags in different races and I got a bit nervy when the first three all won. At that point the rest of the squad came back from the golf course and, realising how near I was to a few bob, joined me in my room. It was bedlam as the fourth race got under way and I must admit I feared the worst when general manager Willie Waddell put his head round the door to find out what was going on. I was still a relatively new boy in the camp and I wasn't at all sure how "Deedle" would react to me betting the horses and, more to the point, the rest of the troops cramming in to the room to find out how I was doing. But I shouldn't have worried — Mr Waddell walked in, took off his jacket and joined with the rest of us cheering on my horse. It was called Weth Nan and was the favourite and you could have heard the roar back at Ibrox when it crossed the line ahead of the field. I was happiest of all, though, because I totalled my winnings up to £567 and I've never won that much since.

Maybe I took it as an omen because it was around then that I really began to feel we could win the League and, for that matter, the League Cup. We were a couple of points clear of Aberdeen in the championship race — Celtic, happily, weren't in sight — and the aggregate victory over Dons had put us in the quarter-finals of the other competition.

Indeed, the only disappointment was the fact that FC Twente knocked us out of the European Cup Winners Cup. We beat Young Boys of Berne in the preliminary round despite Derek Johnstone being sent off in the away game but we found the Dutch harder and couldn't break them down in the first game at Ibrox. That left us with an uphill struggle and even though Alex Miller missed a penalty over there we didn't deserve anything other than a 3-0 defeat.

But on the domestic front it was a different story. We reached the League Cup semis by beating Dunfermline comfortably enough, but we couldn't say the same about our semi-final opponents even if they were lowly Forfar. We got the fright of our lives at Hampden that night and we were within a few minutes of being sunk altogether before we got a grip in extra time and eventually ran out 5-2 winners.

It was an astonishing game to play in because at one time we looked to be on our way with no real problems. Derek Johnstone gave us the lead midway through the first half but they equalised virtually on the stroke of half-time and from their point of view the timing could hardly have been better. Mind you, they didn't complain a lot when they went ahead either and it was only a late, late show from Derek Parlane that took the game into extra time. By then I was playing no further part in the proceedings — DP actually went on for me — but Alex MacDonald, Parlane, then Johnstone again wrapped it up.

There have been many occasions before and since that Rangers have struggled against supposedly inferior opposition but seldom has a side from the lower divisions looked quite so impressive against us. At the end of the night we were only too pleased to have survived it all. And the 5-2 scoreline, we were the first to admit, was hardly a true reflection on the way the game went.

That win came two days after I had helped us celebrate my birthday by beating Motherwell at Fir Park with yours truly scoring our equaliser after we found ourselves 2-0 down early on. When 'Well scored their second goal there was a pitch invasion and we had to go off the field for a few minutes while things were sorted out. The break must have affected the home side because when we restarted we were all over them and in the end won 5-3.

We maintained our run and in the middle of March beat Celtic 2-1 in the League Cup final. That gave me huge satisfaction but more of that later. Our League form continued to be too good for everyone else and we duly clinched the title when we beat Motherwell 2-0 in front of a 47,000 Ibrox crowd on the last day of the championship. Colin Jackson and Gordon Smith scored early goals for us and there was a massive celebration on the terracings when the final whistle went. We had won the championship by two points from Aberdeen.

Our own partying, however, had to wait while we turned our attentions to the third leg of what would be a magnificent treble. Our Scottish Cup run had been fairly uneventful and we even survived a third round tie at infamous Berwick before going on to dispose of Stirling Albion, Kilmarnock and Dundee United on the way to a Hampden clash with Aberdeen. Dons were our fiercest rivals all season and we knew it would be a very difficult final.

We prepared for the game down at Largs at the Marine and Curlinghall Hotel and it was good to get away from the pressures that inevitably build up in Glasgow. It was all quite relaxed and the only panic throughout the build-up came when coach Joe Mason lost his match suit at midday on the day of the match. To be more accurate he didn't so much lose it as it was stolen by Colin Jackson. While everyone else was occupied elsewhere "Bomber" went in to Joe's room and took away the suit. When it was time to head for Hampden we all trooped on to the bus and waited for the off. Time was marching on when Joe appeared in a shirt and tie — and old tracksuit trousers. He wasn't best pleased and even less so when we all looked up at the hotel roof and pointed out his best gear hanging from the television aerial. Silly things like that break the tension a bit and we went on to win the final 2-1.

Alex MacDonald opened the scoring around the half-hour mark and Derek Johnstone added the second, while Dons scored late on through a Steve Ritchie goal that will be best remembered for Peter McCloy's hanging-from-the-crossbar routine. I'm still not sure what the big man was up to at that point but happily it didn't

The theory is fine in training at the Albion as I beat Stewart Kennedy watched by the rest of the lads. Happily, this squad put all we learned into practice during a glorious treble.

matter because we held out quite comfortably and while the final whistle ended the match it also signalled the start of the treble celebrations.

Winning the League Championship, the League Cup and the Scottish Cup was a magnificent achievement and we wanted to mark the occasion in a fitting fashion. So a few of us decided to head out of town into the Lanarkshire countryside to have a meal. In fact, we all met up at wee Tam McLean's house in Ashgill and headed on to the Popinjay Hotel in Rosebank. The party included Peter McCloy, Bobby Russell, Tam, big Tam Forsyth, Gordon Smith and myself with the wives and, in my case, girlfriend. But before we went to the hotel we adjourned to the local bowling club. I'm not sure if they had ever seen a celebration like it but everyone seemed to enter into the spirit of things. It was a tremendous night and after the meal we went back to Tam's house where the party continued until the early hours.

There were several reasons for our successes that year but if any one thing gave Jock Wallace more pleasure than anything I would say it was that we did things in a bit of style. His treble-winning team of a couple of years' previously had done brilliantly but there was always a suggestion that it was power rather than poise that helped the lads lift the trophies.

Jock never went out of his way to really deny that but he didn't have any need to in the 1977-78 season. After all, any side that included players like Tommy McLean, Bobby Russell, Gordon Smith and I could hardly be relied on to power our way to enough victories to lift all the prizes. And for me it was Russell who was definitely the outstanding player of that memorable season.

The wee man joined Rangers straight from junior football — Shettleston Juniors — after being rejected by Sunderland. How the Roker Park club must have come to regret that decision! He was absolutely brilliant in the middle of the park throughout that year and his silky touches made him a joy to play alongside. Bobby was a regular all through and it was fitting that he finished a glorious season by being named man of the match in the Cup final against Aberdeen He displayed his full repertoire of skills that afternoon and, believe me, it was a sight to see. But having said all that the last thing Rangers were at that time was a one-man band. There was skill and ability all through the team and as with most successful sides we laid the foundations at the back. Players like John Greig — who incidentally created history by winning his third treble that year — Tom Forsyth, Colin Jackson, Sandy Jardine and Alex Miller were all good experienced professionals and that gave us a base to work from. Stewart Kennedy and Peter McCloy between them did well in goal and it always meant that we were never in danger of losing too many goals.

If things are relatively secure at the back it gives any team enormous confidence to go forward and our midfield at the time was ideally balanced to cause problems for any opposition. Bobby Russell was, as I have said, an inspiration and Alex MacDonald was the perfect foil. "Doddie" worked and grafted away throughout and also popped up with a few vital goals. Tommy McLean proved yet again that there were few better dead-ball experts in the country and Gordon Smith had a fine first season at the club. It was a team which could get goals from all over the place and most of the lads weighed in with a few, but the man who got most was Derek Johnstone. His power in the air was legendary and of his 25 League goals plus 13 in the other competitions a fair percentage of them were headers.

As for my own season it's only fair to say I didn't set the heather

40

Our experienced players went on to do well after they finished playing. Here I have a laugh in training with Alex Miller, Alex MacDonald, Tommy McLean and Sandy Jardine . . . all now managers.

on fire. I knew when I went to Ibrox it would take me a while to settle in and a variety of other people confirmed that to me when I got there. I had some good games and obviously I did enough to stay in the side in all but a handful of matches but I knew better than anyone that I was playing nowhere near my full potential. If I had been in school my report card would have been marked: "Satisfactory but can do much better."

I was happy enough though. I had won three medals in my first season at the club and that wasn't bad going. Put it this way, if anyone had suggested that around 4.45 pm on 20 August 1977 — the day we were beaten by Hibs in just our second League fixture — I would have sent them off to the funny farm. Never in our wildest dreams did we imagine we could do so well with a side that included three new players in myself, Russell and Smith.

But it wasn't all plain sailing that year. It never is in football and there were bad moments. The worst, undoubtedly, was the tragic death of Bobby McKean in March 1978. He had been at Ibrox since 1974 and was popular with the lads. His death was a terrible shock to us all.

In a completely different way we were stunned at the end of the season when out of the blue Jock Wallace resigned as manager. The first I knew of the Big Man's decision to quit came when I read the news in the morning paper one day in May and there's no doubt it was an absolute bombshell in the football world. He had just led Rangers to the treble and was at the peak of his career. It seemed inconceivable that he should just turn his back on it all. Yet the news was there in black and white and I immediately 'phoned Bobby Russell to see what he thought about it all. Like me, he was flabbergasted and was virtually speechless which wasn't like him.

It's a strange thing that in circumstances like that people always expect the players to know quicker than anyone but generally we're the last to hear and certainly this was one such instance. All sorts of thoughts ran through my head after I got over the initial shock and since Jock never explained why he quit — and still hasn't after all these years — we can only guess at the reasons. One, without question, was money. Rangers did not pay well at the time and clearly Jock felt he deserved more in view of his tremendous success rate. The club, presumably, felt he didn't and rather than have an interminable stalemate Jock got up and chucked it all. I daresay there were other factors and questions have always been asked about how he and Willie Waddell got on but for me it boiled down to basic, straightforward finance. It was no surprise, though, to see Jock immediately go down south and become manager of Leicester City where he did well and had a few good seasons before coming back north to first Motherwell and then, incredibly, Rangers again.

What was a surprise, however, was the instant appointment of a new Ibrox boss.

The directors hardly let Jock out of the door with his belongings

Altogether now . . . follow, follow.

before they took John Greig from the dressing-room and installed him in the big manager's office. Greigy didn't have far to go between the two but it might as well have been a million miles, such was the tranformation between playing and captaining the side and becoming gaffer.

It was a move that sparked even more controversy and from my point of view it did not prove to be a success. Jock Wallace had bought me and clearly rated me. John, as it turned out, didn't appear to share that opinion quite as strongly and we didn't really hit it off when he went "upstairs".

Chapter Four

MY MANAGERS AND ME

I WASN'T sure about how John Greig and I would get on as manager and player from the start because I could foresee him having problems making the switch. And as far as I was concerned my initial reaction could hardly have been more accurate. I'm not particularly knocking Greig because I've been long enough in the game to realise that it could not be easy for anyone to make a move like that and that every manager has a player or players he fancies more than others. But I would say Greigy played favourites more than Jock Wallace for instance. His time in charge at Ibrox was frustrating for me and when you consider he was there for more than five seasons you can maybe see it wasn't the greatest time of my career.

Yet it all started off quite well and in his first season "upstairs" John won the Scottish Cup and the League Cup and came within an ace of the treble. In fact, we lost the League Championship when Celtic beat us with only ten men at Parkhead after Johnny Doyle was sent off. But in the Scottish Cup we disposed of Motherwell, Kilmarnock, Dundee, Partick Thistle and finally Hibs after three games. In the League Cup we beat Aberdeen in the Hampden Park final.

It was a good season but from a personal point of view there were times in it when I realised I might not be flavour of the month as far as the new gaffer was concerned. I was given an early indication of that when I wasn't included home or away against Juventus in the European Cup in September. Yet I could hardly argue for Rangers won 2-1 on aggregate against a team that included a who's who of the Italian World Cup squad. Zoff, Cuccureddu, Cabrini, Scirea, Causio, Tardelli, Gentile and Bettega were all there. It was the same story when I was substitute in the next round against PSV Eindhoven at Ibrox and then didn't play at all in the away leg. But once more Rangers produced an outstanding aggregate win.

Still, that and other incidents proved to me that however brilliant tactically Greigy was in Europe I didn't figure largely in his plans for that type of fixture.

The next season was a disaster for the club — as it always is when we don't win anything — and with the manager introducing John MacDonald more and more it was the same old story for me. The longer this went on the more frustrated I became and I accept I became a bit casual in my approach to everything. I got a bit sloppy in training and when I found myself on the bench I don't think my attitude was all it might have been. I would go home at night after games when I was taken off and substituted and actually begin to wonder if I could play the game at all.

But I had enough self-confidence to quickly get over the depression and put it out of my mind. I'm not being big-headed when I say if anyone had confidence in my ability it was me! That confidence meant I never for a second thought about demanding a transfer or anything like that. There were never any showdowns or tantrums.

Anyway, it wasn't so much the fact that I was in and out of the side that bugged me as much as the way I discovered I wasn't going to play in a certain match. I would realise by the Wednesday or Thursday prior to the Saturday that the writing was on the wall. At that point in the week John would stop speaking to me and simply walk past me in the corridor without a word. It was always the signal that I wasn't going to play and I know other players found the same thing at the time.

Then, and this was another thing that irritated me, when the time came to finally tell me I was being left out he would send coach Joe Mason down to let me know. I would have preferred the news to come straight from the horse's mouth so to speak.

In the end, and after five seasons during which we won the Scottish Cup twice and the League Cup twice, John finally quit as

John McClelland, a tremendous Ranger, leads us on a League Cup celebration lap of honour.

the pressure mounted all around him. Those triumphs might have been enough for most clubs in the same space of time but it is never enough for Rangers. League titles are the measure of success and we didn't have one to show for all the effort so John went.

Yet even if he and I didn't particularly hit it off as manager and player he did have any number of things going for him. He was good tactically as several European results proved and he bought players like John McClelland and Jim Bett. The big Irishman was a tremendous signing when he arrived for £90,000 from Mansfield Town as a virtual unknown and by anyone's standards that had to be a good bit of business. He was a tremendous inspiration and captain at the club and there's no doubt in my mind he was badly missed when he left for Watford a few seasons later.

Bett I had heard about, funnily enough, way back in my school days when we both played in Hamilton. I was a bit older and people would tell me about this young lad Jazzer Bett who looked as if he might become a player. Sure enough he did. I only met him for the first time sitting in the Ibrox dressing-room the day he signed for Rangers. But from that minute on our Hamilton backgrounds ensured we became close friends. And what a smashing player he is. We have played in the same club team and for our country and it has been a pleasure for me to be alongside him on all these occasions.

So you had to take your hat off to Greigy for signing players like them. But the bottom line, and it's nobody's fault, is simply that every manager has guys he likes and some he's not so keen on. I think I fell into the latter category with John Greig.

But that's certainly not something you could say about me and Jock Wallace. I first came across him when I signed for Rangers and I went into the talks with a kind of mixture of fear and awe. He didn't let me down either for I came out again recognising that it wouldn't be in my best interests to ever step out of line and cause a problem. Yet we established an instant rapport, for in that same meeting big Jock said to me: "You don't give the ball away very often, do you?" And I answered:"Only when I want to." He appreciated that and it was the start of what I like to think proved a long and fruitful partnership. Jock was a man's man. If you were straight with him he would be straight with you and that counted for a lot.

In my first few weeks at Ibrox though, I discovered the harsh realities of life under big Jock. His training stints at Gullane, for example, were legendary but while they were hard you felt fantastic afterwards and by the end of the season when the legs were still going strong you appreciated it even more. I wouldn't for a second criticise Jock's training methods even though other people have done regularly.

I have always believed there was a lot more to Jock Wallace as a gaffer than many thought. He always did his own thing and while he respected other people's opinions he would stand or fall on his own judgments. He also treated everyone the same way. In that first spell as boss he had senior players such as Colin Jackson and Alex MacDonald alongside mere novices like myself and Bobby Russell yet we were all the same in his eyes. He had no favourites or at least if he had he didn't show it.

That first season I had at the club was the perfect chance to get to know him and see at first hand just how good a manager he was. His sheer presence was an inspiration for a start but if there was one overriding thing he had going for him it was his power of motivation. Jock didn't really bother too much about tactics simply because he didn't have to. His ability to motivate players game by game was such that that alone was enough. He would talk to players individually if necessary and then collectively and would

47

get us into the kind of mood where we felt we just couldn't let him down. That was the case whatever the occasion but I have to say that it showed more than ever before an Old Firm match. Jock would get everyone going before a Celtic game even more than he would for any other. I for one loved it! And he would never bother unduly about the opposition whoever it might be. He would get us in the dressing-room and tell us we were much better players than they had in the other team otherwise we wouldn't be here. He was always telling us that. And in case we were in any doubt about it he would remind us at half-time although the message might be pitched a decibel or two higher.

He was always talking football and if you were walking back from the Albion training ground a few yards ahead of him he would catch you up and make a point or two in his own inimitable style. There was never any let-up. But at all these times he was straightforward and blunt to the point where some people probably considered him rude. There was many a time, too, when he would give a player a real going over but the great thing about him was that two minutes later he would be back to normal. There were no huffs and no bearing of grudges. I think all the lads appreciated that.

I had my moments with him like everyone else of course and he always told me that he wished there was no half-time in games. That way I would be on his side of the park right next to him for the full 90 minutes and if I looked as if I was drifting out of the action I was handy for a quick roar from the dug-out. Personally, I was always happy with the rules that made it 45 minutes each way.

Another thing that helped him win the respect of the players was that he would never criticise any of us in public. He might have a go in the papers at the team in general but no one was ever singled out publicly and while it might be a small point it didn't go unnoticed in the dressing-room.

He would shield us from pressures as much as he could even if it meant him taking the brunt of the flak himself. The public demonstration that went on outside Ibrox after just the second game of the championship in season 1977-78 was a good example. Everyone felt down and a bit flat and we knew we would get some stick but he deflected it all on to himself and never allowed that catastrophic start to the title race get to us. We kept our pattern and our plan, worked away at it and of course it all came right, which must have given him tremendous satisfaction.

Certainly, he never got the credit he deserved at the end of that

I can't wait to get my hands on the goodies and Gordon Smith and Sandy Jardine look as if they're ready to lend a hand. Jock Wallace is just out of camera shot waiting for his share!

season. People underestimated Jock's ability because any man who guides a team to one treble is good. Anyone who does it again is great. And the astonishing thing about it all is that he did it with two basically very different teams. The first was always acknowledged to be a powerful, strong side and the second better in terms of skill and ability. Yet between them they won all the domestic trophies twice.

Frankly I don't see how anyone can argue that Jock was not a great manager. But, having said that, I'm not sure returning to Ibrox wasn't a mistake as far as he was concerned. They say things are never the same second time around and I guess that was proved accurate in his case.

Yet from a personal point of view I was well pleased when he was reappointed after both Alex Ferguson and Jim McLean had turned

49

the job down in the wake of John Greig's departure. I had unquestionably let myself go a bit because I felt I was getting a bit of a raw deal under Greigy. I know that was wrong and very unprofessional but that was the way it was. I had lost my way and was drifting aimlessly along, not getting any real pleasure from playing. Yet the minute Jock stepped back through the doors at Ibrox he helped me back on the rails. He got me fit again by ordering me to lose five pounds in a month. I lost that surplus weight in a week.

While we won the League Cup twice during his second "reign", though, there was perhaps something missing and I suppose there was a certain inevitability about his leaving again. But I would hope that from a Rangers point of view he will always be recalled with fondness and delight by supporters, for there is no doubt in my mind he did wonders for the club. He's also had successes elsewhere and however it goes for the Big Man in the future I for one wish him well.

In between Greig's departure and Wallace's arrival for the second time I also played under temporary boss Tommy McLean. Wee Tam, a team-mate for long enough, had been Greig's assistant manager and I had come to respect him a great deal in that role so I didn't have any qualms about him taking over even if it was only for a brief spell. In fact it turned out to be just four matches but such was the impression he made in that short time that most of the lads would have been delighted if he had been appointed full-time. Tam had a great way of getting his message across, but don't get the idea that because he's on the small side he was short on ways of letting you know his opinion. He could shout with the best of them but you always knew there was a point to it all. He had a tremendous ability to change things if they weren't going right and, for that matter, improve them even if they were. Tactically he was the best of the three of them and since he left Ibrox he has proved that he always had what it takes to become a very good manager. I'm delighted for him.

Looking at this trio of gaffers, though, tactics were Tommy's strong point while motivation was Jock's and knowledge of the European scene probably Greigy's. They all had a bit going for them and I learned something from each so I'm grateful for that.

But throughout the basically lean years — by Rangers standards — there was one thing I would like to clarify and it's always irritated me for some reason. There were many occasions when the team was playing badly that I played well personally, yet that

Another training session over, thank goodness. Ian Reford and I return to Ibrox from the Albion training ground.

factor never seemed to be noticed. I was singled out by some fans who picked on me and seemed to blame me for the team's performance without ever really looking too closely at my contribution. I was given quite a hard time and I have always felt that was a little unfair. The only justification I can come up with is that for a while I was the only internationalist in the side and maybe for that reason I stuck out a bit. But, whatever, it is something that grieved me and it's good to be able to get it off my chest!

Chapter Five

OLD FIRM BATTLES

WHEN the legendary Bill Shankly said football wasn't just a matter of life and death, it was more important than that, he must have had an Old Firm game in mind. There simply cannot be another confrontation like it anywhere in the sporting world. It is a quite extraordinary 90 minutes when a stadium, a city and a country is divided, and when there is that kind of pressure on you losing just doesn't enter your head.

I've been in a few Glasgow derbies now and it's a strange thing that the more I play the more I want to beat Celtic. At the outset when I first came up against the Parkhead side I obviously wanted to win but the feeling has grown and grown and it's now virtually an obsession. I know all sorts of people will say that is nonsense and how can a game of football affect you in that way. But all I can say in reply is that they can never have experienced the build-up, the occasion itself and the aftermath.

I grew up as a Rangers supporter, of course, and when you do that a victory over Celtic in whatever competition is something to be treasured and valued. The same, I'm sure, goes for Celtic fans who like nothing better than to see their team put one over the old enemy across the city.

It's a strange phenomenon and while other cities might have derby games nothing quite matches an Old Firm one. There are big games between the Milan teams, AC and Inter, in Italy, and similar meetings in Manchester, London and across the world but the ingredient a Rangers-Celtic clash has that the others don't is, unfortunately, religion. That makes it a whole new ball game quite literally and when things are as intense as that it puts this match apart.

It is sad, of course, that religion should enter into sport and I for one am no bigot. I have any number of friends who are Roman Catholics and we go out and enjoy each other's company. There is never any suggestion of hassle. And while I try to steer clear of the religious implications in an Old Firm match I suppose everyone gets caught up in the general atmosphere. You realise some people simply want to see the Protestants beat the Catholics or vice versa.

Me? I just simply want to beat Celtic at every opportunity regardless of whether they have a team full of Mormons, Protestants, Muslims or atheists. My reason is simply that I play for Rangers and Celtic is the enemy in a football sense. There is no more to it than that. There are players on the Celtic side who feel the same way and Tommy Burns, for one, has never hidden the fact that he dislikes Rangers intensely. Tommy, a good player, is a tremendous competitor in these fixtures and like me he thoroughly enjoys scoring goals for his side. He probably has a scoring ratio about the same as me but they are always a bit special in this particular match. Mo Johnston scored a bit more regularly but he took special delight in netting against us and there were a few times when I could have seen the pair of them far enough. Not that I can really blame them because we all get more excited than usual about goals against each other.

Maybe things like that are down to the tension of the game and that makes it perhaps more understandable if not acceptable. Players are always so tense during an Old Firm match simply because they are frightened to lose. The aftermath of defeat in a Rangers-Celtic game is not pleasant. On one hand you get your own fans giving you stick for being beaten by your main rivals and on the other you get Celtic fans gloating and winding you up because they've won. It seems like everyone in the world wants to give you abuse for one reason or another and I rarely go out the house the night we've suffered at the hands of the Parkhead side. It simply isn't worth it.

This kind of atmosphere ensures that players of the two clubs can never really be the best of friends. Sure, we get along in the main but I don't think I could ever go out socially for a couple of

Taking on Brian McClair before the striker moved on to Manchester United.

beers with a Celtic player. It's just not done. We are drawn together at a variety of functions and we get along fine. Mo Johnston and I, for instance, were involved with the same company and promoted their products on any number of occasions and everything always went well. But when it was finished Mo would go off and do his own thing and so would I.

Celtic players and Rangers players also obviously meet up with each other regularly on international duty and there is never any hint of friction. We are with our country for a common cause and in circumstances like that there is no room for problems even if

Taking on Peter Grant and leaving him stranded.

anyone wanted to cause any.

I have, generally, great respect for the Celtic players I have come across over the last decade. They are guys who have reached the top of their careers, who live for Celtic Football Club and who have been fine ambassadors for their team and their country. One such player who immediately springs to mind is current Parkhead captain Roy Aitken who is guaranteed to give 100 per cent for his side. No professional could fail to be impressed by Roy's determination and dedication — apart from when he plays against us — and any youngster would do well to copy his career.

Ironically, I have a lot of time too for Roy's predecessor as Celtic skipper. I have come into direct opposition to Danny McGrain more often than I care to remember and always enjoy these meetings. The first time I encountered Danny was actually when I

I have tremendous admiration for Danny McGrain and Roy Aitken but I don't think it was reciprocated here as I celebrate a goal with Ally McCoist.

was playing for Clydebank against Celtic and I felt I did quite well on that occasion against a guy who was vastly more experienced than me even then. Since that time I reckon I have had my fair share of good games against him as well.

But throughout all that time I haven't half cursed the Parkhead full-back. Danny, particularly at the peak of his career, was one of those full-backs who always liked to attack and he was forever going off on an overlap. Now that didn't suit me at all because it meant I had to chase back with him and whatever attributes I might have chasing and tackling are not among them.

Over the years those two Celtic players have impressed me more than any others. What has never impressed me about their club, though, is the Celtic ground. I've already said elsewhere that I really have never enjoyed playing at their stadium and nothing will get me to change my mind about that.

Celtic seem to have done bits and pieces to Parkhead over the years without ever having made any radical improvements. It seems to have been a case of a few quid here and a few quid there when they might have been better to sort it all out in one fell swoop. I've never felt comfortable with the pitch there either but then again in view of who I play for maybe I shouldn't expect to enjoy Parkhead.

It's maybe a little unfair as well because I am always comparing it to Ibrox and there are not many grounds in Britain, never mind Scotland, which come out of that comparison favourably. Ibrox, since Rangers had the vision and foresight to go the whole way, is a fantastic stadium. I have travelled all over the world with club and country and there are maybe a handful of grounds I would say are on a par or better. The Maracana Stadium in Rio de Janeiro is certainly one and it's the most impressive I've seen. The San Siro in Milan isn't too bad either! Like the Maracana, it's vast and imposing. A bit intimidating, too, for the opposition. But I bet none of them has ever hosted anything remotely like an Old Firm match.

Some of these games, obviously, are more memorable than others for whatever reason and certainly there are a few which stick out vividly in my mind. The first was undoubtedly just that — my first Old Firm encounter of the closest possible kind.

It was way back in September 1977 that I got my initial taste of the unique atmosphere surrounding this game. I didn't have any fancy preparations for that Premier League match and instead followed my normal routine of arriving at the ground as late as possible within the manager's prescribed limit. I have never enjoyed sitting around before kick-off and certainly not with 50,000 screaming fans waiting for the action to start. Indeed, it was that incredible volume of noise that made me realise what it was all about. That and the unbelievable atmosphere that seems to hang round Ibrox, Parkhead or Hampden when an Old Firm game is on.

And that unbelievable atmosphere became even more unbelievable when we went two goals down to a Jo Edvaldsson double inside half-an-hour! It was an amazing scoreline at that point because we had been playing really well yet they had had a couple of breaks, gone up the park and scored twice. We felt a bit aggrieved when we went in at half-time to face Jock Wallace and I think it's fair to say he wasn't deliriously happy either. The gaffer told us that since Celtic had scored two lucky goals we had better go back out and score three bloody good ones.

We knew then we could get back into the game and win it and sure enough that was how it worked out. We kept our heads and produced a terrific second half during which time Gordon Smith scored twice and Derek Johnstone got another to give us a memorable victory.

It was an amazing debut Old Firm match for me and I think it was only afterwards that I fully appreciated just how much is at stake for the teams on these occasions. That 90 minutes action clearly determines how some people will live their lives for a while and I don't think it's any exaggeration to say that.

From our own point of view it was a particularly significant win, coming as it did after a dreadful start to the season for Rangers. We had lost the two opening games when there were demonstrations against the manager yet that 90 minutes turned our season round. It put us back in tune with the supporters and provided us with the base from which we moved on to win everything in sight. That's the kind of effect victory in an Old Firm game can have and I'm sure Celtic could point to similar occasions.

That same season, in the January match, there was an astonishing incident that lads like Roy Aitken and Peter Latchford will no doubt remember with some anguish. We were ahead 1-0, thanks to a brilliant Gordon Smith goal, when Colin Jackson appeared to push Joe Craig in the back. It looked, to be fair, a certain penalty but the referee ignored Parkhead claims even though virtually the whole team surrounded him complaining bitterly. At that point we took a quick free kick and confronted what was left of the Celtic team in the shape of Franny Munro and Latchford. It wasn't a contest and it was left to John Greig to tap the ball in to make it 2-0. In the end we won 3-1.

At the end of that same 1977-78 season we met Celtic once again in the League Cup final. We prepared, as was our custom, down at Largs. There's no doubt in my mind you have to get away from Glasgow before big games like that. You relax in a way you simply wouldn't be allowed to back in the city and it's a good thing for players to realise a cup final or the like is a bit different to the run-of-the-mill League games.

On get-away-from-it-all trips like that the squad inevitably splits into groups who do their own thing. We are all in it together, don't get me wrong, but you simply don't get 16 guys all wanting to do the same thing at the same time. Then, I teamed up with Bobby Russell and we would put in the occasional game of snooker while the likes of Alex MacDonald, Sandy Jardine and Alex Miller would be an inseparable trio. Look at them now, mind you. They are on very opposite sides of football in Edinburgh but I know they're still the best of pals.

Big Tam Forsyth and Tommy McLean always formed a partnership, then as now, and we always joked that the former was only there to be a minder to the wee man. Then there was Colin Jackson. It didn't matter where in the world we were he was always

A goal I'll never forget. It's the 1977-78 League Cup final and Derek Johnstone jumps to it as I connect perfectly with Alan Sneddon and Roddie McDonald unable to do anything about it.

looking to get into mischief. I learned the hard way never to leave my room key in the outside of the door when "Bomber" was about. The first time I did I didn't recognise the room when I went back.

As for the game itself we were never in any doubt we would win it. It didn't come at a particularly good time of the season for us because we were beaten by Aberdeen around then and in fact were beaten by Celtic thereafter. But as far as Hampden was concerned we knew we could do it even if we didn't expect to have to go into extra time.

It was my first final, of course, so that made it special for me right away and when I scored the opening goal of the game I went berserk. It's just as well the gates were closed or I would have been off and running towards Ibrox. That goal came after 38 minutes when Gordon Smith did well to cut the ball back from the line. Derek Johnstone was just in front of me in the penalty area but when I saw the cutback I gave him a shout and after he jumped over the ball I caught it perfectly. It was a sweet, sweet feeling.

But that feeling changed to utter depression later on when Jo Edvaldsson, who made a habit of scoring against us, equalised late on. It was a case of ecstasy and agony in the same 90 minutes. However, with Derek Parlane and Alex Miller on for myself and Johnny Hamilton we scored the winner through Gordon Smith with just a few minutes of extra-time remaining.

After it was all over we adjourned to Ibrox where the Club always put on food and drinks in the famous Blue Room, win or lose, and then players drifted away to celebrate with friends and relatives. I teamed up with Christine and the family and we headed for the Avonbridge Hotel in Hamilton which was my regular haunt.

It was great to win that first trophy and it started me on the way to a record-equalling total of six League Cup medals along with former Celtic favourite Billy McNeill. And unless he makes a shock comeback as a player there I have a fair chance of passing him!

There were a few outstanding memories on the day and one unquestionably was the look on manager Jock Wallace's face when the final whistle blew. I was sitting alongside the gaffer on the bench and it made it all worthwhile to see him at the end. I was also able to give a bit of stick to Celtic's John Dowie who was a Hamilton lad like myself and whom I knew from our days in schools football.

But what that victory did more than anything else was make me hungry for more of the same. It certainly whetted my appetite for more medals and more wins over Celtic.

I was a winner again over the Parkhead side the following year in the same tournament although this time at the semi-final stage. And what a controversial game that was, with my good self to the forefront in the controversy.

Celtic took the lead through Johnny Doyle early in the match but we equalised midway through the first-half with a goal that caused absolute bedlam. I picked the ball up on the right and moved into the Celtic penalty area. Just as I hit it past a Celtic defender I realised I had hit it too far and when we brushed against each other there did not seem anything really in it and nothing whatsoever to get too concerned or worried about, so I was as amazed as anyone when the referee awarded a penalty.

I really found it awfully difficult indeed to believe my good luck while, not surprisingly, the Celtic players went loopy all around me. Tommy Burns was particularly incensed and as he made for the linesman he stepped over me and deliberately stood on my ankle. Unfortunately for him, the referee saw the incident and had no alternative but to send him off.

Sandy Jardine duly scored from the spot when all the furore had died down and we eventually won 3-2 after unlucky substitute Jim Casey put through his own goal in extra-time.

Looking back on the penalty controversy I can only say in my defence that the penalty award wasn't of my making so not down to me although it certainly helped us win. Bearing that in mind — and it is important — then you can see why I was pleased, no, delighted. Celtic players would be just the same.

Being a winner in games like that is great but equally being a loser is no fun and I had to suffer that indignity a few months later when we lost a League game — and the Championship — to our fiercest rivals. One thing would have been bad enough but the two together was unbearable. I really didn't want to face the world afterwards.

We went into that match at Parkhead needing only a draw and when John MacDonald put us ahead early on there was a definite feeling of "here we go". Then Johnny Doyle, who had no love for Rangers, was sent off and that feeling increased.

But just as you're dreaming of glory, football has a habit of giving you a sharp reminder that nothing can be taken for granted and goals from Roy Aitken and George McCluskey did just that to us. Even then, Bobby Russell scored an equaliser but a tragic Colin Jackson own goal and another from Murdo MacLeod right on the final whistle killed us off. It was not one of the great days of my life and on the contrary probably the worst of my career. It was a real horror show.

After a result like that there is no escape. However hard you try to get away from it all a Celtic victory is like a spectre haunting you for weeks.

I was haunted for different reasons a year later when a joke George McCluskey goal in extra-time gave Celtic a 1-0 Scottish Cub Final win over us. It wasn't the result that bothered us most. It was the sickening trouble at the end of what had been a good game. We were all consoling each other in the bath when we learned of the scenes outside and it was a tragic end to the day. There is no place in football for the kind of things that went on that afternoon.

That game will always be remembered principally for the aggravation afterwards but the League Cup Final of season 1982-83

61

will be recalled for one entirely different reason. The Final was on December 4, but a couple of days earlier manager John Greig caused uproar when he signed former Ibrox star Gordon Smith on loan from Brighton. It was a remarkable decision so close to a major match and I don't think it went down well in certain circles. It also put enormous pressure on Gordon himself and made it very difficult for him. So it was no surprise, and I'm sure Gordon would admit it too, when it just never worked out. We lost the match 2-1 and Smudger went back south quicker than expected.

The following year's League Cup Final did work out though — and how! Jock Wallace was back in charge after Greig resigned and we went into the game with the kind of determination to succeed that the Big Man so insisted on. As a result, we went two up through Ally McCoist and even when Brian McClair pulled a goal back we weren't too concerned. But when they scored with a penalty right on the final whistle I thought the end of the world had come. It was a devastating physchological blow to us and exactly the opposite for Celtic who had come back from the dead and were given a massive lift.

Jock, though, kept at us in the brief interval before the start of extra time and eventually a clumsy tackle by Roy Aitken on McCoist allowed Ally to complete his hat-trick and give us a well-merited win. That was another fair old night back at Ibrox and the gaffer had organised a group and a buffet for everyone in the Member's Suite so the place was jumping late into the night.

Old Firm matches without some controversy are undoubtedly the exception rather than the rule and there was enough of that particular ingredient in an encounter at the end of the following season to keep people going for ages. Unfortunately I was one of those right in the midst of it all in front of a 40,000 Parkhead crowd who seemed to quite enjoy my discomfort.

The drama started as early as the second minute, when Roy Aitken missed a penalty, and then continued unabated for the rest of the match. My own particular problem came after I was "done" by Peter Grant. I was far from happy about the tackle and lost concentration briefly. Perhaps if we had steered clear of each other for a while I would have cooled down a bit but instead the opportunity to get even presented itself about 30 seconds later and I duly took the bait.

Predictably there was only one thing the referee could do and off I went after seeing red for the second time in just a few minutes. This time, however, it was a card of that colour that prompted an

A goal against Celtic is something to be savoured and I liked this one although Pat Bonner, Tom McAdam and Danny McGrain don't look as if they appreciate it as much.

early bath with the jeers of the Celtic hordes ringing in my ears.

We were 1-0 down and I was pondering my stupidity in the Parkhead bath when the door opened. That's it, I thought, beaten by Celtic and I'm partly to blame. Ally Dawson wandered in and just as I was about to ask where the rest of the troops were he admitted he had been ordered off as well.

So there the pair of us were and when we heard a huge roar near the end we accepted that the worst had happened and that Celtic had made it 2-0. Ally put his head round the dressing-room door for confirmation only to be told by a stunned Parkhead steward that we had equalised through an Ally McCoist penalty. We were hardly in a position to celebrate but we did allow ourselves a quiet smile each.

Those smiles were bigger than ever in November 1985 when we limped into an Old Firm match with a dreadful run of results behind us yet we beat Celtic 3-0 at Ibrox. It was one of those nights when everything came off for us and we should actually have won even more convincingly although most of the lads were happy enough with the final scoreline secure in the knowledge that Celtic hadn't been outplayed quite as much for a long time. I scored our second goal in that game and I must admit I get a special thrill every time I net against Celtic. I can remember them all as if I was watching action replays on a video. But without question the one that sticks out most of all against the Parkhead side happened in the Drybrough Cup final at Hampden in August 1979. I can recall it as if it were yesterday. I collected an Alex MacDonald cross, flicked the ball up and over Roddie MacDonald, beat Murdo MacLeod and Tom McAdam then did the same to Alan Sneddon as I had done to MacDonald before firing a good shot past Peter Latchford. It was a once-in-a-lifetime effort yet funnily enough we scored another memorable goal that day when Sandy Jardine of all people raced the full length of the pitch leaving Celtic players trailing in his wake before beating Latchford.

Those were the kind of moments that make it all worth while because for a Rangers player there is nothing quite like victory over Celtic. I know it's the same thing for them when they beat us and while one swallow doesn't make a summer and one result doesn't make a season it sure helps.

Beating ex-Celt Murdo MacLeod as Peter Grant looks on . . . admiringly (?).

What did I say about enjoying a goal against our old rivals? This says it all.

Chapter Six

RALLYING TO THE CAUSE

RANGERS supporters enjoy those victories over Celtic but I'm quite sure that if we ever played in the North Pole there would be fans watching whoever the opposition was. In fact, if that was the venue they would be polar bears as opposed to teddy bears!

More seriously, the follow-follow brigade seem to find their way to wherever Rangers happen to be. We have played pre-season friendlies in far-flung places, we have had world tours that, as the name suggests, have taken us all over the place and we have had top-class matches in all the European competitions. Yet I can honestly say I can't remember a game anywhere where there have been none of our fans in attendance. That, of course, merely underlines what most people know . . . Rangers supporters will follow their team to the ends of the earth. And some of the games we've played seem to have been held around that area!

But for all that it's always great to have a few friendly faces around the grounds and, more to the point, hear some good old Glasgow voices yelling their support. We're naturally used to that at Ibrox and although the fans have been known to shout things other than encouragement there's no doubt they are worth their weight in gold.

From a personal point of view I have had a few ups and downs

Just some of the trophies I have collected over the years.

with our massive support but I'm happy to be able to say more of the former than the latter. Like other lads at Ibrox I have been delighted to receive any number of awards from our supporters' clubs that are scattered in all corners of Scotland and beyond. Among the many beautiful gifts I have been presented with are different types of crystal, onyx, trophies, shields, radio-cassette and even a snooker cue.

The awards nights at the clubs are always good fun but sometimes they are not without incident. I recall one evening Christine and I were guests of honour and a young lady came up to me to ask for my autograph. That was no problem obviously but when she showed me where she wanted me to write my name it caused a bit of embarrassment! Still, it's all in a day's work.

But I'm far from being alone in getting player of the year awards and most of the first-team squad at Ibrox receive them. Terry Butcher is highly popular, for instance, and in past years people like Bobby Russell, Gordon Smith, Colin McAdam, John MacDonald and John Greig plus a host of others have all been honoured. The lads try to get to as many of the functions as possible. Jock Wallace always insisted on that and, for that matter, he was usually to the forefront when it came to the singing near the end of the night. John Greig, oddly, didn't attend very often after he became manager but there were always players on hand to go and maintain close links with the legions of fans.

I actually had a long-distance award a couple of years ago when I went to Australia to receive the Player of Year presentation from the Melbourne Rangers Supporters Club. In fact, I didn't go there specially — I was there with the Scotland squad for the World Cup play-off match against the Aussies. A couple of weeks before I left, the troops in Melbourne wrote asking me if they could use the opportunity to make the presentation and naturally I was delighted.

In due course they met up with me in the hotel in Melbourne and gave me a lovely shield which still has pride of place in my living-room at home. They also took the chance to get some photos and autographs and Scotland manager Alex Ferguson weighed in with his presence as well. Even though he was Aberdeen boss at the time the lads enjoyed meeting him and the whole thing went off very well. The same squad of fans, indeed, appeared at a few of our matches in Scotland last season and I recognised the faces.

Like I say, they get to some far-flung places and we always meet up with loads of fans when we play in Europe as well. I remember trips to play Euro ties in places like Cologne, Turin and Eindhoven when Bobby Russell and I might find ourselves with a couple of hours to go shopping. We would be strolling down some quiet street when out of the blue — if you'll pardon the expression — would come a bus-load of supporters.

While it was always terrific to have that kind of backing I did have one particular occasion when I wasn't exactly flavour of the month. Yet it was through no fault of my own and I have always been a bit sore about being made the villain of the piece. The incident came when I was asked by the Rangers Supporters Association to be their guest of honour at the annual rally they hold in Glasgow. It's a big night for the Association's members and while it's not a player of the year thing as such, they ask one of the lads to be the main guest and he in turn is expected to make a speech.

Now, you'll realise by this point that public speaking is certainly not my strong point and while I was honoured to be chosen I made that known to the Association's representatives. There's no way I would have the bottle to stand up and speak to 3,000 fans and I explained that fully, stressing that no slight was intended whatsoever. That was fully a month before the event and I thought that was the end of it until I heard that the committee were asking around to see what suitable gift they could get me for my part in the proceedings. This worried me a bit so I went to see Jock Wallace and he said he would accept it on my behalf and not to worry any more.

That was the last I heard about the whole affair until the *Daily Record* got me out of bed about midnight on the night of the Rally to ask why I had snubbed the fans. Apparently it had been announced to the supporters that I had been delayed on my way there. I couldn't believe it — they knew I wouldn't be there. I was raging afterwards because it was all the talk for a while and I got terrible stick for the episode simply because no one ever told the proper story and I never got my chance — until now — to give my side of the tale. It upset me, and as far as I'm concerned I was the scapegoat for other people's failures.

That incident apart I have always had a pretty good relationship with the fans and long may it stay that way. Those same supporters backed me to the hilt, for instance, when I had a major contract problem with Rangers at the end of season 1984-85. It was a messy time in my Ibrox career and the whole saga was very disappointing from my point of view.

It began when my existing contract with the club was due to run out and, ironically, it followed hard on the heels of a similar case with John McClelland. The big Irishman was a marvellous influence on the team, both as a defender and as captain, and it had seemed inconceivable to the players and the fans that Rangers would allow him to get away. Yet, after John presented his case for what he wanted, the club wouldn't change from their traditional wage structure and the parting of the ways was a bit acrimonious to say the least. John duly went to Watford when negotiations failed completely and he's done brilliantly there, and for Northern Ireland, ever since.

None of this augured well for my own plans for the end of the season, and when Rangers didn't show any inclination to open talks with me I wasn't exactly encouraged. Indeed, that was how things stood until near the end of the season, when Jock Wallace and chairman John Paton called me to a meeting to hear what I thought I was worth. Even though my mind cast back to a previous contract encounter when I signed for Rangers and when I felt I was a bit hard-done-to I still don't think I asked for anything then that was out of order. Indeed, it was peanuts compared, for instance, to the John McClelland situation but the response was a bit negative.

I then had another couple of meetings when we talked round the issue but I have to say that for long enough we were miles apart in our respective views of what I might be due. In fact, I got the distinct impression that they weren't bothered whether or not I stayed with Rangers. I found it all a bit disturbing and certainly not what I wanted to hear. They had already let one internationalist go, in the shape of McClelland, and it seemed to me they wouldn't concern themselves if another followed suit. That was obviously the impression the public at large got about the whole thing as well because I started getting letters and it's no exaggeration to say that 99 per cent supported me.

The Press — always a handy weapon — also weighed in with their views and I was pleasantly surprised in view of my "Moody Blue" reputation to find out they were wholeheartedly behind me too. They clearly believed it was time Rangers changed their policy and who was I to argue!

Yet the club didn't seem in the mood to budge at all and it was a bit depressing, to be honest. The irony of it all is that at no time have I wanted to leave Rangers. Maybe they even knew that and used it to their own advantage. But, whatever, they allowed the matter to drift on and on and eventually my contract ran out and I was actually a free agent.

Christine and I went on holiday up north and for a fortnight anyone who could have tracked me down would have been perfectly entitled to talk to me and, for that matter, sign me. I was astonished that Rangers would allow the situation to get that far but I was stuck with it and the papers were full of talk of me leaving for pastures new.

England, Germany, France, Italy and Belgium were mentioned as possible places for me to end up but while I was flattered at the various interested clubs being mentioned I never fancied leaving. I had seen top-class players like Kevin Keegan and Tony Woodcock go to Germany, for example. Both had done really well for themselves. I had heard, too, about guys going to play their football and pursue their careers in Italy. All of them made huge sums of money — far and away more than I had even dreamed about, far less asked Rangers for — but it didn't particularly impress me.

I am as ambitious as the next man but money isn't my god. As long as I have a few bob in my pocket I'm quite happy. That's always been the case and always will be as far as I'm concerned. People told me before the contract wrangle, during it and since that I could have gone almost anywhere and set myself up for life. But I can honestly say I am not dominated by the prospect of being rich. I guess I'm comfortably off. Certainly no more than that and I'm happy with my lot.

So it was a bit ironic when all the talk was of these other clubs that it was the serious threat of a Newcastle United move for me that provided the impetus Rangers needed to do something positive. Maybe it was just coincidence but it was the day after that United speculation that Jock asked me back into further talks. I believe the rumours prompted a compromise because that's what we ended up with. I didn't get what I wanted or what I thought I deserved but Rangers no doubt paid more than they felt they should have so at the end of the day honours were more or less even I suppose.

It was all a bit untidy and unsatisfactory but one other person who had followed the drama with greater interest than most was John McClelland. He 'phoned me at regular intervals to see how it was all going and, funnily enough, he always used to say he thought his experience would help me. John was still a bit disillusioned by his own treatment and while I guess I had made a bit of a breakthrough it certainly wasn't all that dramatic. It was all a bit different to a previous change in my contract around 1980 for that moved through without a harsh word.

That same summer I "signed" another contract, although this one was for life! In June — the 23rd to be precise and I had better be in the circumstances — I married long-time girlfriend Christine McMeekin. She and I had been together for years and we tied the knot at a ceremony in Coatdyke Congregational Church in Airdrie before going on to a reception at Silvertrees Hotel in Bothwell. After that we managed a few days away at Dunblane Hydro and then headed to start work on the house in Motherwell where we've been ever since.

Chapter Seven

PLAYING FOR SCOTLAND

PLAYING for Scotland has never been a matter of life or death to me since I first represented my country at amateur level all those years ago.

I know that sounds bad and I appreciate that most kids and, for that matter, any amount of adults would give their right arms to wear the dark blue jersey. I understand that myself. Don't get me wrong — I was honoured when I was chosen then and I'm still delighted to be selected now, but if it was ever a case of club against country then I believe I'm duty-bound to go for the people who pay my wages week in, week out. It's just the way I am and while other players might expect and anticipate representative honours I never consider the possibility. If it happens, great. If it doesn't, well, there's no point in losing sleep over the matter.

But despite that apparently callous way of looking at it let me say I have always enjoyed playing for Scotland since I was picked for that Under-18 amateur squad. It was my first taste of the big time, although I don't suppose it was really so big time. Nevertheless, we were treated well, taken to the best hotels and looked after generally as if we were very important.

I played a few games at that level before joining Clydebank and stepping up to the Under-21s. Again, that was a terrific boost and around the same time I had guys like Roy Aitken, Willie Miller,

In scoring action for Scotland against Luxembourg from the penalty spot . . .

Dave Narey, Ian Wallace, Frank McGarvey and George Burley as team-mates.

In all, I played six times for the Under-21s — four when I was at Kilbowie and twice after I moved to Ibrox. In one of those matches, against Czechoslovakia at Tynecastle, I came across a lad called Ondrus who was just about the biggest guy I've ever played against. He should actually have been in their senior squad but was suspended and in among the youngsters.

Despite the presence of the Incredible Hulk we won 2-1 through goals from Burley and Paul Sturrock and I was well pleased with my contribution. I know better now, of course, but just as I was giving myself an imaginary pat on the back into the dressing-room walked my Rangers manager Jock Wallace. "You were brilliant," he declared and just as I thought he was going to give me a day or two off as a reward he added: "Make sure you're at Ibrox early for training tomorrow." How to come crashing back down to earth in one easy lesson from the Big Man. But it was all part of the learning process and I found the involvement with the Under-21s a great experience.

Andy Roxburgh was around even then and I think that's where he picked up the organisational experience he still uses today. Andy was terrific with us and one way and another never let us get at all bored.

. . . and a goal with my RIGHT foot. No, this isn't a case of mistaken identity.

Sometimes when you're away with squads time can lie a bit heavily on your hands but Andy to his credit ensured that never happened. He would organise, say for argument's sake, six tables and get three of us to a table. On it would be a board game like Subbuteo and we would play away quite happily for hours, moving round the tables to the different games. It wasn't all that serious, of course, and there would be a fair bit of stick flying about, but it all helped pass the time.

Andy, in fact, would make sure every minute of the day was accounted for and that was no bad thing. He worked on the theory that we should all stick together as much as possible so that the better we knew each other off the park the better we would get on together on the pitch.

It made sure there were no cliques and he obviously put a lot of time and effort into ensuring everything was just right. Incidentally, that included meal times for, inevitably, there would be a bar of chocolate lying at the side of your plate. He reckoned glucose was important, so there it was. He would also ensure *Flower of Scotland* was played on the tape on the bus just as we arrived at Hampden or wherever. He wanted to see a bit of patriotism and if that worked for just one player then it was a good idea. It's just another indication of how thorough he was and no one could ever fault him for that. His attention to detail was unbelievable. It helped make us feel important at the time and we had some good results on the strength of it.

After that experience I drifted out of the international scene for a while and it was easy to see why. I had quite sufficient on my plate trying to establish myself with Rangers and, believe me, that was a full-time job with no distractions necessary.

It wasn't until September 1979 that I picked up the threads again, when Jock Stein chose me for the friendly international against Peru at Hampden Park. It was my first senior appearance so naturally I was a bit nervous. After all, when you're playing alongside players like Graeme Souness and Kenny Dalglish if they say pass the ball, you pass the ball.

It was also the first time I met the man who was to become my club manager. He "celebrated" our introduction by setting up a great chance for me when he went to the line and cut back a terrific ball. I met it just right — well, not quite right — and it hammered off the bar to safety. I think he reckoned I should have scored but he never said too much.

I was a bit disappointed as well, mind you, because it would have been a bonus to net in my first appearance. As it turned out I was taken off and replaced by John Wark of Ipswich Town but I don't think it was because of that miss. I think Jock Stein simply felt I had done enough in my first match at that level.

There were only just over 40,000 at Hampden that night. It was a good evening for me, though, and in the end a 1-1 draw wasn't a bad way to start my international career. But one thing irritated me and, indeed, the rest of the lads. At this time players' names were printed on the back of the Scotland jerseys. Credit where credit's due and the SFA have come up with any number of good ideas over the years . . . but this wasn't one of them. Apart from anything else it made it easy for the fans to spot who made a blunder! But it wasn't just that. It was a crazy idea in general and to make matters worse the names used to start peeling off the strips halfway through a game! Happily, the plan was scrapped pretty quickly.

The next international was against Austria and this time, just a month after the game with Peru, it was the real thing of the

Graeme Souness set up this chance for me on my international debut against Peru. Maybe he was right — I should have scored when you see where the 'keeper is!

European Championship. Obviously I had hoped to keep my place in the side but I wasn't too disappointed when I was named among the substitutes. Jock naturally enough went for experience and this was the starting line up: Alan Rough, Sandy Jardine, Gordon McQueen, Kenny Burns, Iain Munro, Graeme Souness, John Wark, Archie Gemmill, Arthur Graham, Kenny Dalglish and John Robertson.

Hans Krankl opened the scoring courtesy of a slip by Rough but Gemmill equalised and I got on for a piece of the action in place of Graham. And 1-1 was how it ended. The European Championship then as now is not a happy hunting ground for Scotland. We have never been particularly lucky with the draw for the tournament and certainly we've never done very well. It's strange in view of the tremendous results we get on our way to qualifying for various World Cup finals. That same season we were later beaten by Belgium — them again! — home and away and eventually finished up behind the Belgians, Austria and Portugal in a very undistinguished fourth place in the five-team group.

So our Euro hopes ended and so too did my international career for a while at least. It wasn't a particulary inspiring spell for me anyway and I had enough to do trying to get a game for John Greig's Rangers without worrying myself too much about playing for Scotland. For some of the time my attitude to football wasn't right anyway, as I've explained elsewhere, so there's no way I could complain about not getting a game for my country. But I always believed that if you're doing the business for your club you would get the chance again and that's how it turned out. It is no coincidence that my return to the international arena in February 1984 came after Jock Wallace replaced Greig at Ibrox. The Big Man got me going again and just a few months after he went back to Rangers I was back in the international plans.

The game was a British Championship fixture against Wales at Hampden and while it was my return it was Mo Johnston's debut. The striker was with Watford then and earning rave notices down south. And when he hit the winner in that match it was easy to see why. He looked very sharp but it wasn't a bad occasion for me either. I actually opened my goal account for Scotland from the penalty spot after Paul Sturrock was brought down, though I have to be honest and say it wasn't one of the world's great spot kicks. On the contrary, I didn't hit it at all well and although Welsh 'keeper Neville Southall dived to his right and seemed to be set to save it the ball crawled under his body. As it happens, it wasn't all that different to a rather more important penalty in a World Cup qualifying game a couple of years later but more of that at the appropriate time. Robbie James scored for Wales but Mo's goal did the trick and it sent the small crowd home relatively happy.

The one thing you couldn't call the crowd at my next international was "small". That was against England and over 70,000 squeezed into the national stadium to see the 1-1 draw. Mark McGhee scored for Scotland and Tony Woodcock equalised with a terrific strike for the English.

By rights I might not have been playing in that match for Rangers had fixed up a world tour which coincided with the England game and a match against France that was to follow. But Jock Stein and Jock Wallace worked out a compromise that allowed me to play at Hampden and then join up with the club thereafter.

John McClelland was in the same situation for he was chosen to play for Northern Ireland, so the two of us were left to get on with it. That might have been all very well if we had been going across the country to Edinburgh. But in fact we were going across the

Not a soul in sight but Richard Gough and Paul Sturrock insist on waving to their fans! I get on with the business along with Steve Nicol and Mo Johnston.

world to Australia! Still, we made it more or less in one piece and that was a bit of a miracle in itself. And when I heard Scotland had been beaten 2-0 in Marseilles I wasn't too upset I had missed the occasion.

I wouldn't however, have liked to miss the friendly against Yugoslavia the following season, for Scotland cantered to a 6-1 win and I was on the scoresheet again along with Graeme Souness, Kenny Dalglish, Paul Sturrock, Mo Johnston and Charlie Nicholas.

To be fair, they looked an awful side and defensively they were a shambles. Not only that, when they were really up against it they threw in the towel and didn't want to know. Eventually they were just going through the motions and it was all a bit unreal. Still, no one was complaining too much and we all thoroughly enjoyed ourselves.

I played in front of Jim Bett that night and that has always been a pleasure for me. We are firm friends, which helps, and room-mates, which sometimes doesn't! If I was running a book on it I would put our room at about 2-1 on for being the most untidy in any Scotland squad get-together. I won't say we leave clothes and things lying around but it once took Jim ten minutes to find the

The terrible twins . . . Jim Bett and I.

Another devastating action shot watched by Jim Bett and Jock Stein.

television. He's a good lad, though, and I christened him "Noisy" which is the exact opposite of how he really is. He says so little but when he does speak he's an unconscious comedian.

For all that we have a great understanding on and off the park and when it matters most I know exactly where Jim is going to play the ball and vice versa. That developed at Ibrox when we were team-mates and hopefully benefits Scotland.

Our mutual understanding was probably shown to its best advantage that night but in another friendly against an Iron Curtain side, East Germany, in October 1985 Jim wasn't playing and nothing was particularly impressive anyway. It was a disappointing 0-0 draw and there really wasn't much to get worked up about.

At the end of that season we went to Holland to meet The Netherlands in Eindhoven and although it was once again a no-score draw it was a fine effort from Scotland. We had gone there with what was virtually a Premier League squad because of English club commitments and only Andy Goram and Arthur Albiston stopped it being an all-tartan team. Ally McCoist got his chance that day and we did well enough overall.

The match has always stuck in my memory for another strange

reason. It is the only time I have represented Scotland abroad apart from when I played in a World Cup qualifying game in Spain and in the finals in Mexico. I suppose wingers like myself are a bit of a luxury away from home and that statistic certainly seems to back up the argument.

The thing about playing for Scotland is that I have always felt I had to prove myself in every game. I suppose some people will think that is fair enough but the feeling extends to training sessions and it is completely different to anything I have ever experienced at club level.

I realise and accept, naturally, that you always have to do your best but there is a bit of added pressure — quite a bit — involved when you are with the international squad. You are constantly looking over your shoulder — not literally — at who is next in line in the queue to take your place. There is competition for places that is obviously more intense than it is with the various clubs. From the manager's point of view it is presumably a good thing but from the player's side it can be a bit overwhelming at times. Still, if you can't stand the heat get out of the kitchen, and that applies quite nicely here. I can handle pressure as well as the next man and I can honestly say that I wouldn't have missed the experience of playing in all those internationals for anything. I have had some marvellous times, been to some great places and met some terrific people.

Within the Scotland camp itself there has been a variety of characters I might never have come across but for my international involvement. And top of that list, without any doubt or the slightest hesitation, is Jimmy Steele.

"Steelie" has been Celtic's masseur for longer than probably even he would care to remember and he's provided the same service for Scotland players over the years. He is the Mr Fixit — Jim'll Fix It — of the international squads because anything anyone wants the first place to head for is Steelie's room. It's a veritable treasure trove of goodies, with everything from Radox for the bath to a stick of chewing gum. You want it, Jim has got it. And if by any miracle you stumble on something he hasn't got to hand he'll soon get it! He's a bit like Arthur Daley in *Minder* really. The lads all love him for it. Everyone I have seen pass through an international squad has been able to get on with Steelie and the place simply wouldn't be the same without him. Being a Rangers player I am in the ideal position to give him a bit of stick here and there but, believe me, he gives every bit as good as he gets. The

Celtic lads are always winding him up to push a cream cake into my face and when he opts out at the last minute he gets terrible abuse from the likes of Mo Johnston and Roy Aitken. It's at that point that they call him "Squeak" and ask him if he's a man or a mouse. He keeps the lads going from the minute we all get together.

Steelie, incidentally, also does a few pretty good — not great, just good — impressions and one he does about a mythical Czechoslovakian coach is absolutely brilliant. Another one he does, "Tam the Tipster", is clever as well but while he takes the mickey in that one there is a serious side to his tipping of horses and I'm delighted to say he's pointed me in the right direction occasionally. By the way, he also carries out his professional duties very well and his rubs before a match are legendary. Others, such as Eric Ferguson of Dundee, Donnie McKinnon and Hugh Allan, have been involved in the backroom support side of things and I've found them all very helpful.

On the coaching side I have to mention that I had a spell with Scotland when Jim McLean was assistant to Jock Stein. Now that was an experience. The Dundee United manager has a remarkable track record at Tannadice where a pitifully small support is constantly fed some marvellous football. Outstanding players have come and gone — I'm thinking of people like Andy Gray and Richard Gough — yet Jim somehow still manages to turn out terrific teams. His achievements with United are phenomenal and no one can ever take that away from him. But, and here's the crunch as far as I'm concerned, I'm just glad he never took the Rangers job when it was offered to him a few years ago. I can't believe he and I would have got on. I don't think I'm the kind of player he would have liked to handle and certainly I wouldn't have relished being a player in his side. I'm the first to concede I'm a bit inconsistent and I think that would have led to a fair share of bust-ups between us. And I couldn't handle things like the "warm-downs" United have after a match when the players have to go back out to a deserted ground and go through exercises. I daresay they have a genuinely worthwhile purpose but I certainly wouldn't have enjoyed that and other aspects of his managerial style. As I say, I'm the first to hold up my hands in congratulations for what he has achieved in the game, but he and I teaming up? It would have been nothing if not interesting.

Happily, we got on fine in the limited time we had together in a Scotland sense and I think I can safely say that about everyone I've been involved with internationally. After all, you are generally together for just three or four days at the most — World Cup finals apart — and there is no room for hassles or upsets. That applies particularly to the day of the match when players and staff are so keyed up they tend to go about their own business anyway.

On an international match day I always get up reasonably early for breakfast, for instance, but the players are given the option of a long lie and breakfast in their rooms which some take up. After my cereal and boiled eggs — not together! — I might have a leisurely walk around the hotel. When we have stayed at the likes of Turnberry, Seamill Hydro and Gleneagles you'll realise that can take a while. After that it's a normal lunch if it's a night game, and then up to the rooms again for a sleep. I have a bit of a problem there and like a few of the others I find it difficult to nod off so inevitably I'll just lie and watch the telly and then have a quick bath.

By late afternoon it's time to go back downstairs for a light snack which at one time was almost inevitably steak. No chips, potatoes or vegetables. Just steak. But medical opinion nowadays suggests that is too heavy before a game so diets have changed a bit in recent years. I like a simple bowl of tomato soup or maybe scrambled eggs followed by a cup of tea but you do get some other weird and wonderful choices. Some players might have rice pudding, others maybe go for peaches and a few might have boiled or steamed fish. Basically you can have what you like as long as it is light.

After that, by the time we've gathered together all our bits and pieces — and in the room I share with Jim Bett that can be a lengthy process — we're ready to roll. On the coach going to the ground I always organise my tickets. I usually get a few envelopes from the hotel and sort the briefs out for the various members of the family and for friends who'll be at the match. Other than that it's just idle chat among the lads until we get to the stadium.

That's when the pressure really begins to build up, though there's always such a buzz about the place that you don't get too much time to sit and reflect on what might happen. There is a team talk as well and although most of the preparation has been done beforehand the manager will utilise the time to make a specific point about your own game or about the opposition. After that and when you go out on to the pitch the team is essentially on its own.

At the end of the night, win or lose, we generally simply drift away with relatives and mates and look forward, hopefully, to the next time.

It's a myth, of course, to think your few days away with your

Davie two-caps.

country is going to make you a quick millionaire. You get £100 appearance money and a daily allowance of a tenner. I'm not complaining, you understand, just trying to kill the belief that we're all in it simply for the money. There is very much still an element of "playing for the jerseys" about our international set-up and there's nothing wrong with that.

And on that subject, funnily enough, I find I have given away a lot of the strips I've worn. I have handed quite a few over to deserving causes and if they have helped raise a few quid for some charities then good and well.

We actually get two jerseys per match nowadays although that is a fairly recent thing. We have the one we start in and then a fresh one at half-time and we can keep them both. Often, though, the players are involved with swops with a member of the opposition, although that's not a practice I get involved in unless I'm asked particularly.

Having said that, I have a fair number of foreign strips at home including a Brazilian one, Austrian, Peruvian, Welsh, Icelandic, Australian, Dutch and Luxembourg. Oh! I also have a Spanish one which was worn by none other than the Butcher of Bilbao, Andoni

85

Goicoechea. I suppose they are a good keepsake but who ever sees them lying in a bag in the loft?

I also have four caps and again, contrary to public opinion, you obviously don't get one every time you play for your country. Instead, you get one for every season in which you have represented Scotland. You might have played once in a season or six times but you still get only one cap.

Like I say, I enjoy it all whether or not the cap fits but I have never, and will never, consider it to be the be-all and end-all. For me playing for Scotland is the icing on the cake but it's the bread and butter of club football that allows me to live the way I want to and I can never forget that.

Another reward for playing for Scotland ... man of the match presentation to yours truly.

Chapter Eight

TRIUMPH AND TRAGEDY
IN WALES

THE WORLD CUP is different. It is the most prestigious trophy competed for and obviously the greatest tournament I'll ever play in. So even at the stage of the qualifying games just being involved felt a bit special.

The preliminary matches for the 1986 competition began nearly two years earlier and since it was my first taste of World Cup action I felt a little bit nervous, which isn't at all like me. Scotland, as ever, had a difficult section with Wales and Spain representing our biggest threat and Iceland completing the group but by no means there simply to make up the numbers.

It is a myth that nations like Iceland and, say, Luxembourg are cannon-fodder for the better countries. These teams include players who are professionals all around the world and Iceland, for instance, had a smashing player in the shape of Siggi Jonsson, not to mention Jo Edvaldsson, who was well used to the Scottish style from his time in this country.

But it's not only the handful of real quality players they have that takes them to a reasonable standard. They usually have coaches who know the game inside out and can organise them to suit the players' capabilities. And when they play within their limitations it is usually a defensive style that can be very difficult to break down and frustrating to play against. Getting men behind the ball to defend is one of the easier aspects of the game and although you hand the initiative to the opposition it doesn't necessary follow that it makes it easy for them.

It's a bit of a hobby-horse for me the way some of these teams play but I accept their reasons for it. It's just not a type of football that's very enjoyable to play in. It's really all about when you get the first goal against them. If it's early it means they have to come out and play a bit if they have any ambition at all and that in turn makes it a game at least. If you struggle to score then the pressure gets greater and greater, your supporters start to get on your backs and generally the longer it goes without a goal the harder it gets.

So basically we reckoned we were in for a hard time in group seven of the World Cup qualifying competition. What we didn't imagine for a second is quite what a traumatic section it was to turn out to be.

Despite all our misgivings about Iceland we opened our account with a comfortable 3-0 victory at Hampden when I set up Paul McStay for an early strike and the young Celt added a second before Charlie Nicholas finished it off. It wasn't a great game but we were quietly satisfied with the opening result and it set us up nicely for what we knew would be a crunch fixture against the Spanish in Glasgow in November 1984.

As it happened, I believe Scotland produced their best performance of any I have been involved with in the game against Spain. We were brilliant that night. Everything just fell into place and with Jim Bett behind me I believe it was one of my own best performances as well. Every one of us was at the top of his form Stevie Nicol was outstanding, Graeme Souness did brilliantly, Paul McStay was terrific. It really was a privilege to be in the side. We won 3-1 with Mo Johnston scoring twice and Kenny Dalglish getting the other in a style only he can. The Butcher of Bilbao himself, Andoni Goicoechea, got their consolation but it really was no more than that and the 74,000-plus crowd went home well pleased with life.

Manager Jock Stein, too, was delighted with the way we won the tie. Jock never displayed his emotions too publicly but the players knew when he was pleased and most certainly when he was not. That night he had a quiet smile on his face and we all knew we had done the business.

The team, and it's one I'll always remember, was: Jim Leighton, Steve Nicol, Arthur Albiston, Graeme Souness, Alex McLeish, Willie Miller, Kenny Dalglish, Paul McStay, Mo Johnston, Jim

The Bluebell Girls we certainly are not! Richard Gough and I have got the hang of it but Paul Sturrock is out of step. Steve Nicol and Mo Johnston don't quite know what to make of it all.

Bett and yours truly. I was thrilled with my own game and as far as I'm aware Urquiaga, the Spanish right-back, never played again after that, so I must have done something right.

Yet in the midst of all the euphoria I was desperately upset about something else. The weekend before the match Christine's father John died and, in fact, I was late joining up with the squad while I kept her company. It was a very difficult time for us all because we were close. But I knew he would have wanted me to go and play and I'm only sorry he wasn't there to see it. He would have enjoyed the occasion and the performance.

The result put us in a tremendous position with two home games played and two good wins under our belts. The next game was also against Spain — in Seville — and, for a change in a match like that away from home, I was picked to play from the start. Maybe I shouldn't have been too surprised though, for Jock had been glowing in his praise of me beforehand. "Cooper has a reputation in Spain because of his performance against them at Hampden three months ago," he declared. "He knows the importance of playing well and has shown a new responsibility in a Scotland jersey . . . There is no doubt that Spanish manager Miguel Munoz was surprised at what he saw Cooper do at Hampden. There aren't many wingers about like him nowadays." It was a major boost for my confidence — which is probably why he said it — although I was feeling great after the first game anyway.

So we headed for Spain feeling we could take another gigantic step forward, while readily accepting how difficult it would be. No side, be it club or international, travels over there over-confident about getting a result. For years Spain has produced marvellous players and even if our lads had ideas about an easy victory they would have had them knocked out of their heads twice over. Once, most assuredly, by the manager who would never tolerate anything like that. Jock had his feet on the ground at all times and while he was always confident he never took it any further. And the second reason was the venue for the game. It was a measure of Spain's determination to make it as difficult as possible for us that they staged the match away from Madrid. The Sanchez Pizjuan Stadium — ironically where my former manager Jock Wallace was boss — is a spectacular setting. A typical continental ground where the stands rise quickly and where the fans seem to tower above you. Certainly the supporters seemed to be well placed to throw things at us from a great height and if the Scots lads had collected all the oranges aimed in our direction we could have started a marmalade factory.

More seriously, these oranges made a fair old dent in the pitch, so we were a bit concerned what they would do to our heads. Fortunately, no damage was done to life and limb but that, along with the noise that seems to be trapped in grounds like that, meant it was a pretty intimidating night. The natives, you'll gather, were less than friendly and I don't think Jock Stein was too happy about the situation. I know I wasn't!

Yet we carried on where we left off against them in Glasgow and looked quite comfortable. At half-time I remember saying to one or two of the lads that I reckoned the worst we would get in the end would be a point. But that was about as good a tip as my normal picking of horses and a goal from Clos sent us home empty-handed.

It was a disappointment but nothing compared to the home game against the Welsh when we could do nothing right. It was a bit like a Premier League game because, unlike the Spanish, Wales played a similar type of football to ourselves. The poor ball took a battering and a half in the match and there were a couple of ferocious incidents such as the tackle involving Graeme Souness

When Jock Stein spoke, we all listened. Graeme Souness, Steve Nicol and I give the big man our undivided attention.

and Peter Nicholas. The ball sat innocently on the ground between them as they got on with it and it wasn't a pretty sight. In fact, the only time the ball moved anywhere positive the whole night was into the back of our net, courtesy of Ian Rush. The 1-0 defeat was a real setback for us.

But with the group the way it was it wasn't an irretrievable situation and a 3-0 Welsh victory over Spain in Wrexham kept hopes alive and well. It also meant that we needed a victory against Iceland in Reykjavik and that proved to be the one qualifying game I missed. I had a knee injury that ruled me out of the match against England a few days earlier and although I reported to Gleneagles before the fixture against the Auld Enemy I was sent home again when it was clear I wouldn't have a chance of playing in that one or in Iceland. So instead of being in Reykjavik with the lads I was in the local squash club when the action got underway. It wasn't one of the great sporting occasions but I was up in the air with the best of them when Jim Bett, who is incidentally married to an Icelandic girl, scored the only goal of the game with virtually the last kick.

Basically it all now hinged on our last group match against Wales in Cardiff on 10 September, 1985, a date that was to become etched in my mind. There was much talk beforehand about where the game should be played and the Welsh officials, mindful of the Scottish takeover at Anfield in a previously similar experience, eventually opted for the capital.

I was delighted to be back in the squad after missing the previous international but at the same time I didn't hold out too many hopes of playing. Scotland only needed a point and in these circumstances a winger can be a bit of a luxury. Jock, though, named me for a place on the bench and I felt that if things were going against us I might get a chance. At that point, if it was to shape up that way, I thought I might be of some use. But obviously I was hoping in another way that I would not be needed for that would mean Scotland had everything under control.

We were confident that would be the case. Wales were a good, competent side and there's no question they had two tremendous strikers in Ian Rush and Mark Hughes. The pair had formed a deadly duo for their country that was the talk of the football world and we were well aware that they would be the main dangers to our ambitions. On the other hand the Welsh defence was really no more than ordinary and the hope was that we might be able to do some damage in that direction.

So the build-up began in earnest — you can always tell when that happens because everyone in the world seems to want a ticket for the big game — and our preparations were perfect. There were no problems, no hassles on the run-in, and Jock Stein went about things in his usual efficient and meticulous manner.

Unfortunately the best-laid plans etc and while Mark Hughes' brilliantly taken goal might have had them singing in the Welsh valleys it struck a bad note with us. It was a marvellous strike by the then Manchester United star although I don't recall thinking that at the time. What it did was leave us with the World Cup finals in Mexico becoming a distant dream and it wasn't a pleasant feeling after all we had been through.

It really seemed at that point a case of so near yet so far and the huge army of our fans in the crowd were stunned into near silence. That was how things stood at the interval and although Jock looked tense when he talked to us at half-time managers are always like that during a game.

There was, however, a bit of drama in the break when Jim Leighton informed the manager that he was having trouble with

An international line-up, from left to right: Graeme Souness, Arthur Albiston, Paul McStay, Richard Gough, Paul Sturrock, yours truly, Willie Miller and Roy Aitken.

one of his contact lenses. That came as a bit of a shock to everyone, including his club manager Alex Ferguson who was Jock's assistant, for up until then no one knew he wore the things. The announcement certainly caused a flurry of activity in the dressing-room and Alan Rough, who not so long before thought his Scotland career was over, was hastily stripped ready for second-half action. It was an astonishing scene and not quite what we all had in mind for the interval.

Jock, though, singled me out and told me I might be pushed on if it didn't change from 0-1 and although the scoreline wasn't to my liking I was keen to get into the fray. My chance came midway through the half. I was sitting along with the other substitutes at the far end of the bench to the manager. He told Fergie to get me out for a warm-up and after a couple of runs up and down the track I was summoned back and told to get ready. I did so and awaited instructions from the manager. "Go out and play wide on the left. Go at them and try to get behind them as often as possible," Jock told me. I didn't consider for a second that those few words would be the last orders he would give.

I went on, in fact, for Gordon Strachan after initially Stevie Nicol's number had been wrongly held up and I immediately saw quite a bit of the ball. I felt good and early on I nutmegged Joey Jones just to boost my confidence. Then, with about ten minutes left and with Mexico fading even further into the distance, Scotland were awarded a penalty.

There is no doubt in my mind now, and there was no doubt then, that it was a legitimate penalty. I had a grandstand view of the incident when David Speedie tried to knock the ball over Dave Phillips and instead played it against the Welshman's hand. Sure, it was unlucky for him but equally surely it was a spot kick. As the rules stand a handball in the penalty area results in a penalty and that was good enough for us.

I knew straight away that the job would fall to me. Gordon Strachan and I were the nominated penalty takers but since I had replaced the wee man just a few minutes earlier it had narrowed the choice. And just in case there was any doubt in my mind big Roy Aitken wandered over to me with the ball in his hands and told me to get on with it!

I just wish I had a pound for every time someone has asked me since how I felt at that moment. It's not easy to describe exactly, believe me. I wasn't especially nervous despite the bedlam going on all around me with the Scots fans going wild with delight and the Welsh supporters simply going wild.

My initial thought was simply that here we were, just a few minutes from making an inglorious exit from the World Cup and I had a chance to salvage it all. It was all I could think of and it was only much later when I sat at home with a cup of tea that it really hit me. Then, I virtually started shaking at the thought. What would have happened if I had missed it? Imagine being labelled forever with the tag of the man who lost Scotland the chance to go to Mexico. But, as I say, such pessimism never entered my head — possibly because I was so confused there was no room for it! My problem, apart from keeping cool, was deciding where I would place the spot kick. I recalled in a flash the previous time I had lined up a penalty against Wales 'keeper Neville Southall and my wee brain nearly blew a fuse as I tried to settle on whether or not I should stick with my usual habit of placing them to the goalkeeper's right. I remembered that Southall had very nearly saved it last time out when I did that so I opted to change and elected to hit it to his left. This, remember, was all happening in the space of just a few seconds, though it could have been an hour as far as I was concerned.

Eventually, after the 'keeper indulged in a bit of gamesmanship, I stepped up, hit it well and watched in horror as Neville dived the correct way and looked for all the world as if he was going to save it. He did everything — or nearly everything — right, but after what seemed an eternity the ball somehow squirmed over the line.

Roy hit me first and then the rest piled in and it was a glorious, marvellous feeling. I looked over towards the Scotland bench and there were a few people, including Alex Ferguson, on their feet celebrating as well. I never thought too much of it at the time because he never showed too much elation, or for that matter disappointment, but Jock Stein stayed in his seat at that point. Maybe that was significant.

After that penalty we could even have gone on and won the game but it finished 1-1 and the referee's signal to end the match was the signal for us to run about congratulating each other. Fans came on to the pitch, television cameras and radio microphones were thrust into our faces and then, as I got near the dug-out, I came face-to-face with Alex Ferguson who said: "Big Jock has collapsed. We don't know what's wrong. Stay there for a minute."

I turned to tell some of the others to wait and Richard Gough and I stood side by side as throngs of people milled around the end of the tunnel. Eventually we made our way to the dressing-room and Fergie came in and again told us Jock had collapsed. No one said anything else and there was an eery quiet which was only broken when Scottish Football Association President David Will came in. He was crying and said simply: "We've lost the manager. Jock's passed away."

It was a dreadful moment when nothing, least of all a football match, seemed to have any significance. No one moved, no one did anything. Every man had his own thoughts although few could actually understand fully what had happened. Alex Ferguson then returned and he was distraught. He talked to us briefly about the manager and then tried to get everything organised. In fact, he was remarkable in the circumstances.

We were all still in our kit and it was some time before players moved off to the bath and generally made a move of any sort. But still there was almost total silence. In due course we sorted ourselves out into some sort of order and made our way out of the stadium to the bus where groups of fans stood around obviously only too well aware of the tragedy. The worst moment, and there were many bad ones as you would expect, came when the coach pulled away from the stadium and I asked myself what we were doing leaving when the gaffer was still there.

It was no different at the airport for we were all overwhelmed at the sadness of the whole thing. Jimmy Steele, who knew Jock better than most, was naturally worst affected because of that and he was inconsolable. His eyes were red and Alex Ferguson gently steered him over to where Paul McStay and I were sitting. "Look after him," said Fergie and we did our best but I am well aware it was probably not good enough. It was difficult enough to think straight but televisions dotted throughout the building kept repeating the news.

The flight home was awful and when we arrived back at Edinburgh everyone seemed to drift away with their own feelings and I left for home with Christine who had come to collect me.

Later, much later that night, I thought back to the evening and briefly considered that I had just scored the most important goal of my career yet it meant nothing really. Football was put firmly into perspective and I think a great many people reflected then that maybe it didn't matter so much after all. But life has to continue and the 1-1 draw had paved the way for us to meet Australia in a play-off while Spain went through in the top position in the group.

We were faced with home and away games against the Aussies and in the first match at Hampden we did enough to have won by several goals but in the end had to settle for 2-0. Alex Ferguson was in charge and there was nothing particularly remarkable about the match. I scored the first goal after Graeme Souness and I lined up a free kick which I eventually hit sweetly enough past the Australian 'keeper. Frank McAvennie added the second, which we were pleased to see go in for 1-0 wouldn't have been all that comfortable a lead to take Down Under.

It was my second trip to Melbourne in a couple of years but it didn't get any easier second time around. It's a long haul and even though we were brilliantly treated in the first-class section it was no fun. I was happy enough, I suppose, because apart from the football I was being given an opportunity to visit a variety of relatives. My mother's brother and his wife and their children and families were scattered all over the city so at least it meant I wasn't short of places to see and go.

Melbourne is a lovely place, anyway, and apart from finding tickets for them all the only problem I had was trying to keep a room-mate! I started off with Paul McStay who caught a 'flu bug and was despatched off to a room on his own. Mo Johnston was called in as "substitute" but then he went down with a virus as well.

I think at that point Fergie decided it was all my fault for afterwards I was left on my own. He wouldn't risk anyone else!

We were in Melbourne for quite a while so we could acclimatise for though it was early December and very cold at home it was the Aussie summer and that, I can assure you, means it's hot. As for the match, we were dreadful although happily not bad enough to surrender our two-goal advantage. We had done the main part at Hampden and it showed. It was a poor performance but we were never in any danger of losing and missing out on qualifying. So we headed home with our sights set on Mexico and the World Cup finals.

It was a marvellous feeling to know we had carried on where previous Scotland teams had left off by successfully battling through to the last stage of the tournament. But the over-riding thought among all the players as we pondered on the possibilities for Mexico was simple and straightforward . . . we had done it for Jock Stein.

Probably the most important kick of my football career . . . but did it really matter in the circumstances.

97

Chapter Nine

MEXICO AND THE
WORLD CUP

EVEN the prospect of the so-called "Group of Death" — as the World Cup section that included Scotland, Denmark, West Germany and Uruguay was nicknamed — failed to dampen Scottish enthusiasm as players, officials and supporters alike looked forward to Mexico '86. That enthusiasm was tempered with cautious optimism, although it must be said there was none of the ballyhoo that accompanied the build-up to the ill-fated tournament in Argentina eight years previously. Instead, there was a realisation that we had done tremendously well to get to the finals in the first place and a fierce determination to maintain the good work when the crunch came.

Nothing was left to chance and well before a ball was kicked in earnest the Scottish Football Association were working out the fine details of our preparations. Much of the work, of course, had been done well in advance but as the competition proper grew ever closer we were measured for clothes and put through a stringent medical check. That took place at Turnberry under the supervision of international doctor Stewart Hillis and basically consisted of nine minutes cycling on one of those work-out bikes. It might not sound too much but, believe me, it took its toll and a couple of the lads failed to finish.

Not that it was in any way a competition. Rather, it was a means

The latest in fashion gear certainly had me in a sweat as I prepared for the World Cup.

99

of Dr. Hillis checking us out in terms of heart, blood pressure and the like in view of the difficulties we knew we would face at altitude in Mexico. The Doc had us all taped — literally — with wires running to our hearts, foreheads, arms and wrists and when we had all finished he looked as if he had enough notes to write a medical book. Happily, everyone was declared fit and healthy when the results of all the tests came back and that kind of preparation brought it home to everyone just how close the finals were.

The Doc also took the opportunity to determine whether or not any of us were taking any sort of medication and that was clearly a legacy of the Willie Johnston affair of 1978. Then, as you may recall, "Bud" was sent home when traces of a banned drug were found in his blood after a random test and the SFA were not about to let the same thing happen again. It was all very thorough and similarly all the cash incentives and commercial aspects of being a World Cup finals squad were ironed out well in advance.

The players got together in a Glasgow recording studio at one point and did the obligatory record. It was called *We're making the big trip to Mexico*, with *They carry the hopes of Scotland* on the other side. I can't honestly recall it ever proving too much of a threat to the Rod Stewarts, Elton Johns and George Michaels of the pop world.

In fact, we didn't do particularly well commercially from the World Cup but that was never a major concern to the players. I can say quite honestly that the last thing on our minds was money-grabbing in the run-up to Mexico. Instead, we concentrated on trying to make the 22 and when manager Alex Ferguson duly announced it no one could have been happier than me to be included. I was, after all, 30 and Mexico represented my only serious chance of playing in the greatest tournament in the game.

Even though I am very much a home bird I was absolutely delighted to be packing my bags and preparing for the big adventure. And talking of packing my bags I reckon I must have had something like 40 T-shirts supplied by various sports goods manufacturers. So medically, sartorially and mentally I was as ready as I would ever be for the World Cup. And so, at that stage, were 20 other Scottish players. The one exception, sadly, was Kenny Dalglish who was forced to pull out through injury virtually on the eve of departure. Obviously there are no bad players in a World Cup squad but Kenny is a bit special and his absence was undoubtedly a blow. Fergie in turn called in Steve Archibald of Barcelona and that was us once more at 22 strong.

The squad was accompanied by the manager, assistant Walter Smith and a back-up team that included the likes of Craig Brown, Archie Knox, Andy Roxburgh, Jimmy Steele, Teddy Scott, Eric Ferguson and Hugh Allan. There was also a host of SFA officials and others but, in the eyes of the country, I suppose it was the players who mattered most and this was the pool that carried Scotland's hopes when we jetted out of Glasgow on 14 May: Jim Leighton, Alan Rough, Andy Goram, Richard Gough, Willie Miller, Alex McLeish, Maurice Malpas, Dave Narey, Arthur Albiston, Gordon Strachan, Graeme Souness, Jim Bett, Paul McStay, Roy Aitken, Steve Nicol, Steve Archibald, Frank McAvennie, Charlie Nicholas, Graeme Sharp, Paul Sturrock, Eamonn Bannon and yours truly.

It seemed a good, experienced squad and if there was a criticism of it at the time then some folk reckoned there should have been a place for Liverpool's Alan Hansen. The big Anfield defender has a lot of admirers and many reckoned he would excel in the difficult conditions in Mexico but at the end of the day the manager can only name 22 players and he is bound to upset people. Some of those left out took it well. Others didn't. Hansen was one of the former and he found the time and the character to wish the boss and the lads all the best. David Speedie of Chelsea, on the other hand, could not contain his disappointment and Mo Johnston was the same. I wouldn't hold that against them, though, for it must have been a desperate disappointment.

Ironically, I was actually with another of the lads left behind when he discovered he wasn't going. Murdo MacLeod of Celtic and I were on a promotional job in Stirling when someone tracked down the midfield man and told him his wife had heard from Alex Ferguson and that she was trying to get in touch with him. We both knew why and instantly there was a nagging doubt in my own mind about whether or not I too would get the dreaded call. But it never came and in due course I was a member of the party that left in good spirits and, I'm sure, with the best wishes of a nation alongside us on the haul to Santa Fe via London, Dallas and Albuquerque.

The only hiccup along the way was on our arrival in the States when Charlie Nicholas was found to have a Libya stamp on his passport but it was smoothed over and caused only a slight delay.

I had my own thoughts on the planes and buses that ferried us to our New Mexico destination and essentially they were the ones that have carried me through my career. I was simply delighted to be part of it all and when I looked around it was obviously a feeling I shared with the rest of the lads. But unlike some I knew I was going to the World Cup probably, at best, as a substitute. There is a place in modern-day football for wingers but there is also a time and I was realistic enough to know that my role might well be confined to the bench and a late run if things weren't going Scotland's way. No one told me as much, but you didn't need to be a genius to suspect it.

Although I would have dearly liked to have been proved wrong it turned out exactly as I anticipated. I didn't see 45 minutes — not even half of a game — action in Mexico. But for all that it was an experience I wouldn't have missed. Apart from anything else, I wouldn't have liked to have missed Santa Fe.

It didn't look a lot when we arrived but after you got to know the people and the place it was fabulous. Our Sheraton Hotel base was perfect. It had a variety of amenities such as sauna, jacuzzi, squash courts and the like and sat on a slight hill overlooking the town that was about ten minutes' drive away and a huge shopping mall that was even closer. If I sound like a tourist, forgive me. And if I tend to go on about the place it's because I enjoyed it so much and, maybe more importantly, it was heaven compared to what followed. The hotel had a huge blackboard in the foyer with all the players' pictures on it and a sign that said: Welcome to the Scottish national soccer team.

Initially, we did very little other than laze about getting over the journey and generally settling in to our new surroundings. For some, that meant lazing by the pool while for others it was an opportunity to do a bit of exploring. Graeme Souness, my new boss at Ibrox, used the time to pick my brains a bit about life at Rangers and it was there he gave me the first hints about what later was to turn Scottish football upside down.

But then the serious work started and, strangely for me in view of my distaste for training, I actually thrived on the twice-daily sessions in the sun. But that was the secret of it because you knew the weather would be good and everything seemed so much better when the sun was on your back. At first it was desperately hard for everyone for Santa Fe had been chosen specifically because it was 7,000 feet above sea level — like Mexico — and what a difference that makes. I actually felt light-headed after a training session. Breathing was difficult and Jimmy Steele spent most of his time pouring fluids down us all. It was a very strange, and uneasy, feeling.

There is always time for a spot of relaxation with my other favourite sport.

The other problem for most of the players was blisters. All the lads had new boots with them specially designed for the World Cup but wearing them in didn't half cause some pain. Overall, though, it was brilliant and Fergie and his team deserve credit for ensuring nothing went seriously wrong.

One of the principal problems facing a squad in our situation is boredom yet Fergie and Co managed to keep us occupied enough without going daft in training as we were hearing the English lads and the Irish players were doing during their build-up. The manager gave us two sessions a day but in between them we were allowed to lie in the sun for a while and afterwards the boss and his coaches would split us up and take us for a meal.

The first time, I went with Jim Bett and Oldham's Andy Goram among others and Fergie took us all to a nice Italian restaurant before we went on to meet up with the rest of the lads who had been elsewhere with one of the other backroom staff for a beer together. It all helped break the routine and fostered a good team spirit and once more Scotland seemed to have learned lessons from Argentina when, from all accounts, the players were stuck together in a camp with nothing at all to do for days on end. We just didn't have that problem. Jim Bett and I even managed to get down to the local cinema and saw *Back to the Future* one night.

Then there were the Race Nights which were right up my street. Andy Roxburgh organised them but the star of the show, as always, was Jimmy Steele. These Race Nights show videos of horse racing on a big screen and everyone gets the chance to back their horse. Manager, players and officials all joined in the fun and Steelie did his Tam the Tipster bit. At one point, and after tipping a series of failures, Jimmy was up on the stage urging one of his nags on. He was like a jockey in front of the screen and, to be fair, it seemed to be working, for his horse was streets ahead until it was overtaken inches from the finishing post. He took a fair bit of stick for that.

He wasn't much better at the real thing either for we had a couple of chances to go to the famous Santa Fe Downs racecourse and with my interest in racing it could hardly have been better. The Downs was a fantastic place and for a poor punter like me who had only ever seen Ayr and Hamilton it was all a bit much. But everyone got into the spirit of the thing and no one was more pleased about that than the bookies!

SFA secretary Ernie Walker would have been better donating his dollars to the bookies' benevolent society. Fergie once said of him: "He could not win an each-way bet on the boat race." Not that the Park Gardens supremo was alone. President David Will put some money on a nag and it was withdrawn at the starting gate! Gordon Strachan talked a good game but he would have been as well betting a donkey on Blackpool beach. I fared not too badly but all things are relative and if I had returned to the hotel with a single dime I would have been well off compared to some. It was a great day, however, and goalkeeper Andy Goram of Oldham and I later returned for a second helping. The bookies were disappointed the rest of the squad didn't go along again as well.

It was all designed to prevent boredom creeping in and on a more serious note — but for basically the same reason — Fergie also set up a meeting with Northern Ireland who were based at nearby Albuquerque. It was an opportunity to give the lads a semi-competitive run-out but I'm not sure the boss was too pleased about it afterwards. For a start we all had to change outside and then, in the midst of a series of mini-games Richard Gough and Irish defender John O'Neill of Leicester clashed heads and the then Dundee United man had to have four stitches put in his wound. It was all really just an exercise in the heat but one plus was undoubtedly the form of Charlie Nicholas. He was tremendous and looked set for a marvellous tournament.

After it was all over I had a chat with former Ibrox team-mate John McClelland and in fact went back to Jimmy Nicholl's room for a shower. I wish I hadn't bothered because I left my boots there and they didn't turn up back at Santa Fe for another couple of days.

Our time in New Mexico generally, though, was well spent. I felt as fit as I've ever felt. The camp was great, the preparation ideal and we were bursting to get on with it. Even the Doc's warning about the possibilities of Montezuma's Revenge — a quaint and very unpleasant little ailment — and Charlie Nicholas' graphic description of what it entails couldn't put us off!

Our next port of call in the build-up was Los Angeles where we were due to play two games against local sides, LA Heat and Hollywood Kickers. We knew the fixtures wouldn't be walkovers for Dundee had just a few days previously drawn with the latter side and been beaten by Heat. The games were a good test and in the first against Heat we won 3-0 through goals from Charlie, a wee Gordon penalty and Stevie Nicol. We went one better — although the goals were scored late on — against the Kickers with Eamonn Bannon, Graeme Sharp, Frank McAvennie and Paul McStay netting.

Maybe, in retrospect, we should have called a halt to the adventure there and then because there's no doubt New Mexico and America were in every sense the highlights of Scotland's summer. But at the time we didn't know what fate had in store and we certainly didn't expect Villa Arqueologica in Teotihucuan that was to be our next base.

The name of the town translates into "the place where men become gods" but it should have read "the place where men become prisoners". It was quickly nicknamed "Colditz". I don't want to be unkind but the rooms were caves. I remember wondering afterwards why we had had a police escort to the place because no one else could possibly have wanted to go there. We were the last nation to arrive in Mexico but if a few of the lads had had their way we would have been the first out.

There was only one 'phone in the hotel and that could only take incoming calls. I had a few bizarre calls from Christine back home and I think the neighbours reckoned she didn't need a phone at all, she was shouting so loudly to try and make herself heard. It wasn't quite the end of civilisation as we know it but after Santa Fe it certainly seemed like it to the players.

Not that we were there to enjoy the trappings of luxury, although in the same breath we could have stood a few home comforts. Still, we had a job to do and although no one was deliriously happy with the situation it didn't for a second interfere with our main aim which was simply to get on with it.

That meant Denmark and we had any number of team meetings leading up to the main event. We knew before we left Scotland, of course, that the Danes were an exceptional side. Their qualifying track record, for instance, was vastly impressive. They were in a group that included Russia, Switzerland, Eire and Norway and they had achieved some excellent results en route to Mexico. Denmark beat Russia 4-2, for example, and throughout their section games the public began to take notice of players like Soren Lerby, Preben Elkjaer and Michael Laudrup. Certainly Fergie had and he recognised their right to be acclaimed one of the most talented teams in the tournament.

On top of that it was generally accepted that the opening game of the competition is one of the most important of all. Win it, and all of a sudden the pressure is off slightly. Lose it, and you are forever chasing the situation as you try to qualify for the next stage. So the manager and the players were well aware of just what was at stake and if we were in any doubt at all about the intensity of the entire proceedings they were finally laid to rest when the serious action kicked off with the first match between Bulgaria and previous winners Italy in Mexico City on 31 May. A crowd of 105,000 packed into the Azteca Stadium for the 1-1 draw and we sat and took it all in not once, but twice. It was a feature of life over there at the time that television showed games live . . . and then repeated them! Still, it gave us a taste of the atmosphere, but the competition really took off a couple of days later when the host nation took centre stage.

Mexico opened with a game against poor Belgium and if ever the odds were stacked against a team then it was on that occasion. There was hardly a friendly face in the ground when the Belgians appeared and it really must have been like entering the lion's den for them. There is phenomenal interest in the national team in Mexico and the whole country ground to a standstill whenever they were involved in ties.

As it happens they won that game 2-1 but it was the aftermath of victory that grabbed most of the headlines the world over. The whole of the country seemed to descend on The Angel which is Mexico City's answer to London's Piccadilly and while at first it was party, party all the way the mood of celebration changed dramatically as the night wore on and eventually it became a riot. If nothing else, it proved to us exactly what was at stake, so we were under no illusions.

As the countdown continued the pressure increased, with Danish boss Sepp Piontek playing his part in the usual war of nerves that precedes big games. Piontek had looked and sounded ultra confident in the build-up but the nearer we got to kick-off so we could detect a bit of apprehension creeping in. It was good from our point of view and helped us settle.

Unfortunately, none of it mattered a great deal to me personally because I wasn't involved. When the manager named the team I found myself on the bench — but fully clothed, not stripped even for an emergency. I was, naturally, disappointed but I wasn't alone and the spirit was such that everyone wished the lads who were playing all the best without any rancour. So this was the side Alex Ferguson sent out against the powerful Danes: Jim Leighton, Richard Gough, Maurice Malpas, Graeme Souness, Alex McLeish, Willie Miller, Gordon Strachan, Roy Aitken, Steve Nicol, Charlie Nicholas, Paul Sturrock.

I'm not the greatest spectator in the world and it wasn't easy sitting through the 90 minutes. I think it's even more frustrating when you're so close to the action yet so completely incapable of doing anything to alter the course of the game. As it was, we played quite well, certainly deserved to draw but instead lost an unlucky goal to Elkjaer and with it two crucial points.

The style we were forced to use through the conditions was so totally alien to all things Scottish that it was always going to be difficult but I don't think anyone fully realised how difficult until after that opening match. Some of the lads lost seven and eight pounds in weight and it was very, very exhausting. It was the same for the opposition, of course, but they are maybe a bit more used to the type of possession play that was so important out there. Possession was absolutely imperative because when you lost the ball you might have to chase around for ages trying to get it back and that was hopeless. You had to work in short, sharp bursts and conserve your energy whenever possible. If you were chasing your tail it inevitably took its toll.

So one way and another it was a very subdued squad who left the Neza 1986 Stadium in Nezahualcoyotl and headed the hour or so back to Teotihucuan where we had a couple of beers. We didn't need telling we had been unlucky but neither did we need reminding that already it was going to be an uphill battle to fulfil our World Cup ambitions.

All the while, naturally, other countries were experiencing the same roller-coaster emotions. By the end of the same night, and after the first few days of the tournament, Northern Ireland had struggled to a 1-1 draw with Algeria and England had been beaten by a Portuguese squad which had been wracked by internal strife since arriving in the country. It was hardly, then, a case of Rule Britannia and although we saw the Press contingent more or less every day we had to rely on 'phone calls from home to determine the mood back in Scotland.

Things at least looked up after that initial setback off the field when we moved headquarters temporarily to Queretaro for our second section match against West Germany. The lads were delighted about that because the surroundings were a good deal better and it helped brighten the mood in the camp, although, heaven knows, the opposition wasn't getting any easier.

Franz Beckenbauer's team, as usual, had had a few upsets on the way to the World Cup but they are so vastly experienced and so well used to doing well in the tournament that it was never going to be anything other than a difficult game.

This time I took a step nearer the action by being one of the substitutes and overall Fergie made a few changes in the side from the team that started against Denmark. Dave Narey of Dundee United was in for Alex McLeish, Steve Archibald was playing instead of Charlie Nicholas and Eamonn Bannon, who had gone on for Strachan in the first game, replaced Paul Sturrock.

Once more we did well and this time got our reward when wee Gordon scored a smashing goal and then provided everyone with a laugh when he went to jump over one of the advertising hoardings in celebration only to decide at the last minute it was too high! He settled for having one leg on top of the board when the troops rushed over to congratulate him.

Not that our delight lasted long, for almost immediately we lost an equaliser when the ball fell into the path of Rudi Voller and he made no mistake. It was an unkind break and we certainly didn't deserve it.

There was, though, worse to follow when Klaus Allofs made it 2-1, but if nothing else the goal that put the Germans ahead at least signalled my first involvement proper in the World Cup. I was sent on for Bannon while Frank McAvennie made his second appearance off the bench, this time in place of Nicol.

It's always difficult when you go on to find the pace of the game and that was once again the case in this one. I thought, mind you, that I did quite well and I set up a chance for Richard Gough but nothing really went right for us and we didn't do too much after that unfortunate miss. I came off at the end feeling as if I had played the whole 90 minutes. I was shattered and the fact that we had lost 2-1 didn't exactly give me a lift. Yet, as with Denmark, we really had faced some quite marvellous players and we hadn't let anyone down. West Germany boasted lads like Schumacher, Briegel, Magath, Littbarski . . . the list is endless. They even had a player like Karl-Heinz Rummenigge on the bench, although, to be fair, he had been injured.

The ironical thing was, however, that we still had a chance of going through even after two defeats. The system is such that a victory from our last game against Uruguay would take us into the next stage. It's crazy really that that could happen but it was all down to the other results and we certainly weren't complaining.

We were very optimistic. We felt to a certain extent we had been let off the hook and we were quietly confident we could take Uruguay who had previously drawn 1-1 with West Germany but had been thrashed 6-1 by the Danes.

During the build-up I learned, via Christine, that the papers were full of speculation that I would be playing from the start and gradually I began to believe maybe I did have a chance of a full game. I wasn't over-confident because it's never been my style to take things for granted and that was just as well.

Jim Bett, basically, felt the same way because he hadn't had a kick of the ball at any stage and reckoned he also might play some part. So the two of us were sitting lingering over our meal the night before the game when Fergie came over to us. It wasn't too difficult to know what he was going to say but when he told us we wouldn't be playing it still hurt a bit. We were undoubtedly disappointed but at least I had the consolation of a seat on the bench again and the possibility of making myself useful. Poor Jim didn't even have that for consolation.

Mind you, maybe he was as well out of it because it was hardly a memorable occasion. This was the side that lined up: Leighton, Gough, Albiston, Aitken, Narey, Miller, Strachan, McStay, Sharp, Nicol, Sturrock. I went on in the second half for Nicol and Charlie Nicholas replaced Sturrock. Neither Charlie nor I could make much impression, however, and by then everyone had seen enough of the Uruguayans to know they wouldn't have let us beat them anyway.

They had Jose Batista sent off after 54 seconds for a horrendous foul on Gordon Strachan who had obviously been targeted as the man to watch . . . and kick. Some people actually reckoned that the French referee pulled out a red card instead of a yellow one by mistake but it was such a ridiculous tackle that Batista couldn't have had any real complaint. What he did do, though, was set the pattern for a ferocious series of assaults on the lads and by the time I went on it was patently obvious it would take a miracle rather than just me to manage a goal against them.

We could still have been playing now and I don't believe we would have scored. I'm the first to admit we probably didn't play well anyway but how can you when you're getting chopped at every turn? They weren't going to concede anything that day come hell or high water. The 0-0 draw was ignominious to say the least and, perhaps not surprisingly, we began to get some stick back home.

Looking back on it now there's no doubt some was justified because we didn't do the business when it mattered in that last game. In fact, we were dreadful. But at the same time I think we can point with some justification to the earlier games when the breaks went against us at crucial times. I'm not saying we would have gone on to cover ourselves in glory and win the World Cup but given an element of good fortune I think we would have ended up giving a better account of ourselves than we did.

Overall, it's difficult to say our failure was down to anything other than the fact we have too few world-class players. It's that simple. How else can anyone reasonably explain it? Our preparation under Fergie and the other coaches was fine, we had excellent information on the other teams, as a squad we all got on well and it's impossible to look at conditions and blame them when you see how France and Denmark, for instance, played.

I would love to be able to say this or that was wrong but I think objectively you have to put it down to the fact that, at that very high level, we were not good enough.

After the Uruguay game, naturally, all everyone wanted to do was get home as quickly as possible. It goes without saying we would rather have stayed on and qualified but when our fate was secured all thoughts turned to going back. There wasn't much time wasted in achieving that aim and we left Mexico to the more successful sides who got on with it quite happily in our absence.

When I did get home I put a few bob on the exciting French side who had looked so good in the early part of the competition, but they lost a daft goal against West Germany in the semis and never recovered and in the end I watched on telly as Argentina beat Beckenbauer's team 3-2 in the final.

I've thought a lot about the World Cup since then and the overriding conclusion I have come to is that I wouldn't have missed it for the world. It was a tremendous experience and many of the things I saw made a lasting impression. None more so than the hovels we saw people sitting outside on our way to the revamped stadium, done up at a cost of millions, in Nezahualcoyotl. There's something not quite right about that. It's difficult, anywhere in the world, to justify the amounts of money spent on the World Cup while a fair percentage of the country's inhabitants were living in squalid, pitiful accommodation. Mexico is not my favourite place.

On the football side of it, Gordon Strachan was probably Scotland's sole success. The wee man seemed to thoroughly enjoy it all and responded with some marvellous stuff, with the highlight undoubtedly being our only goal against West Germany. Others, undoubtedly, did not have a good World Cup. Poor Jim Bett for one. He never actually played but he was twice chosen for the random dope tests. The first time was after the opening game against Denmark when he had to wait for about three hours while Gordon worked himself up to do the business and then again after the Uruguay match. It wasn't one of life's greatest sporting occasions as far as Jazzer was concerned.

Mind you, I didn't exactly cover myself in glory either although in fairness I didn't see too much of the action throughout the whole show. Still, I'm only glad I was able to be involved in it all because, at 30, as I was then, I knew better than anyone that it would be my one and only chance to play in the most magnificent spectacle of them all.

Chapter Ten

MACLEOD, STEIN, FERGUSON AND ROXBURGH

THERE is, undoubtedly, pressure on players who compete at the very highest level of football but I can't believe it compares with the ones who become managers of inter-national teams. It must be a whole new ball game after bossing a club and I put my cards on the table right now and declare I wouldn't fancy it one little bit.

Yet in saying that I have tremendous respect and admiration for the guys who have achieved that status and honour. I have played under four such men for Scotland — Ally MacLeod, Jock Stein, Alex Ferguson and Andy Roxburgh — and it's difficult to imagine four characters more different yet with that one thing in common. But before I delve into their personalities I think it's only fair to point out essential differences between the managing of a club and the managing of a country as I see it.

At club level, the boss sees his players more or less every day whereas in the other situation it can be months between get-togethers. That level of contact and non-contact is crucial and to give you one obvious example of how much of an impact it has a club manager can sort things out immediately after a defeat. Imagine how an international boss feels when he has to wait weeks before he can get his points across about the previous match. That must be the most frustrating aspect of all but the club manager is

Do what I do for Rangers, said Jock Stein. Here's a sample as I take on St Mirren's Tommy Wilson.

also in a more powerful position when it comes to doing or saying something to a player who does, basically, belong to him. At best, a national manager might only have three or four of his own men around him and he has to use a certain amount of tact in his treatment of players from other teams.

Three of the quartet I have been involved with have had these, among other, difficulties and only Roxburgh has not been with a club previously.

But it is to "oor Ally" that I turn first and since you've got this far you'll realise he's not my favourite person nor, for that matter, me his. He struck me from the first moment I met him as being too extrovert for my liking and too excitable for his own good.

It has to be said, of course, that I never actually played under him but I did go on that World Cup fact-finding tour of South America in 1977 and what I saw didn't unduly impress me. He is obviously tremendously enthusiastic — perhaps too much so in view of the debâcle in Argentina the following year — but you have to make allowances for that. Indeed, it's difficult to put a finger on the exact reason why he and I didn't really hit it off.

We certainly didn't get off to the best possible start in view of the story about Jimmy Stewart and I being accused of being late one day but there was more to it than that. On that same trip we were all in the hotel dining-room having a meal at one point when a photographer wandered in and started taking some photographs. His timing could, I admit, have been a bit better but no one was prepared for what followed. Ally got up and launched a tirade against the poor bloke and went really over the top. The players couldn't believe what they were seeing because it really was a relatively trivial thing to get upset about and in view of my early dealings with the media I should know!

His fate eventually was well and truly sealed by the events in the World Cup of 1978 but Ally is nothing if not resilient because he's still a high-profile figure in Scottish football and you have to give the guy credit for that.

It is impossible to imagine anyone more opposite to Ally than big Jock. He was, without doubt, my kind of manager. A guy in many ways like Jock Wallace in that he would call a spade a shovel and if you were straight with him then he was straight with you. He also didn't bother too much about tactics and that was right up my street. Just about the only tactic I know is picking the ball up and trying to beat half a team. He appreciated that. Jock would let you get on and do your own thing to a certain extent and the only advice or instruction he gave me was to go and do what I had been doing for Rangers.

There was, of course, a measure of respect for Jock before I even met him in a Scotland sense. His achievements with Celtic — and I curse them often enough — were enough to guarantee his stature in the eyes of the players and from that point of view he was off to a flyer at international level. He knew everything there was to know about the game and knowledge, in any walk of life, helps a whole lot. Certainly no one I knew ever disputed big Jock's knowledge of football. At team talks he would linger only briefly on the opposition. Just long enough, indeed, to give you the salient points but his message was always that what mattered was the Scotland performance. It was what we did that counted and that alone gave us confidence because we knew he believed in his players.

But while I liked to think I earned his respect and many others did the same it should be pointed out pretty damn quickly that he wasn't a man to be trifled with or messed about. Mixed with the respect we had for him was an element of fear because he was such a big man in every sense. His stature, his achievements and his very presence were awesome. That's why few people ever stepped out of line and if you did, you only did it once. He had this habit of letting you know if you had done wrong in front of all the rest of the lads and there's nothing worse for a player than being embarrassed while your team-mates look on. In fact, that's what he did, he embarrassed you into never making the same mistake twice! He was a master craftsman with a brilliant way of getting to you psychologically and his death in Wales left a huge void in Scottish football.

He would have loved the World Cup finals. Mexico would have been a great stage for him and his presence would have benefited the entire proceedings. But it was not to be and it's desperately sad that he should be snatched away like that in a moment of glory.

The man who succeeded him was Alex Ferguson and that was no easy task in the first instance. Jock Stein wasn't an easy act to follow. But Fergie had a few things going for him that made it easier than it would have been for others. For a start, he had, like Jock, done tremendously well with Aberdeen and his track record at club level was there for all to see and admire. He was also part of a new breed of football managers. Younger men who were closer age-wise to players and therefore more aware, through their own relatively recent experience, of the dressing-room antics that are part and parcel of the game. After all, it wasn't so long ago that Fergie played and he knew better than most what the banter was like between players. Indeed he actively encouraged it. You could always have a laugh with him — at the right time — and I found him easy to get on with and to play for.

His biggest task, of course, was taking Scotland to the World Cup finals in Mexico and I have to say at the outset that I thought he did extremely well in difficult circumstances. He was helped in no small way by the coaches he had around him. Lads like Walter Smith, Craig Brown and the others took as much of the weight off his shoulders as they could. But the bottom line is the boss. He was also aided as manager of Scotland in that he had his own Aberdeen players with him. Jim Leighton, Willie Miller and Alex McLeish especially had tremendous respect for the guy even though they may not always have seen eye to eye with him at Pittodrie. And their presence and their attitude towards him helped make up the minds of other players. These things all help in relationships between an international manager and the players he has at his disposal.

Fergie, though, used to like nothing better than joining the lads in matches after the most serious part of training was over. He revelled in these games and at the end of them he would always want to have a penalty competition. I really can't imagine why because 12 yards was a long-range shot for a tap-in merchant like him! He was murder at taking spot kicks. But if anyone can remember his playing days they'll realise why. Anything out of the six-yard box and he was lost. From our point of view it was a real booster to our confidence to watch him in training! Apart from anything else, if you had been dropped it gave you a legitimate chance to have a kick at him. His game, really, was five-a-sides and if he managed to score a goal even the rarified atmosphere couldn't stop him from doing a lap of honour.

But there is very definitely a serious side to Alex as well and you cross him at your peril. His half-time talks at Pittodrie are legendary and from what I have heard it wasn't unusual for cups — the tea kind not trophies — to be flung from one corner of the dressing-room to another. I've often wondered what people like Bryan Robson and Norman Whiteside make of it all at Manchester United where Fergie is now very much the boss.

Not that he was really in a position to do that with players on international duty but he wasn't slow, believe me, to make his point. He would do that individually or collectively and he is a master at reading a game and knowing whether or not to put on substitutes. He also took time out to explain his decisions to players and whether or not you agreed with them the lads always appreciated being told exactly why this or that was being done. I must say I like Fergie and I really rate him. I'm sure he'll sort Manchester United out and I hope he does.

Similarly, I hope Andy Roxburgh can get Scotland going although, to be brutally frank, I don't envy him the job. To a great many people Andy was a strange choice to be international boss following the World Cup. Andy Who? was the favourite phrase of the time. But why shouldn't Andy have been given his opportunity? Previous incumbents had all been club bosses before their appointments and whatever their individual merits not one — including MacLeod, Stein and Ferguson — had made us into a real force in international football. Certainly, for all their plusses none had made too much of the World Cup, for example, although I don't for a second suggest it was their fault. But they all had a club management background and I agree with Scottish Football Association secretary Ernie Walker who was adamant a change in direction in our national boss was not such a bad thing.

Mr Walker wrote on this very subject in the SFA's annual report and I go along with most of his thoughts. "There appear to be those who insist upon looking for something sinister in the fact that the Association turned to a member of its own staff to fill this job from which controversy is never very far away," he wrote. "It was evident before the appointment was even made that a more 'traditional' choice from the ranks of club managers along the lines of those who had gone before would be more acceptable to some of those with the loudest voices. This suggestion would be entirely understandable if it were felt that Scotland was on the right road internationally and that all that was needed was to bring in someone who would carry on along the path to success. Nothing, of course, could be further from the truth. We appear to be going along year after year without any particular signs of improvement and the International Committee felt that it was high time to try a different tack," he added.

I was really quite interested in all that and even more so when he went on to list previous managers with club management backgrounds and commented: "Not one of them was acclaimed as being outstandingly successful in the job. Some of them, of course, from time to time, chalked up some excellent victories and we did qualify for four World Cup finals during the latter part of the period but nevertheless the point has to be made that at no time since we started entrusting the affairs of the national team to one man have we achieved the level of competence and consistency which every Scotsman fervently desires, not to say demands. Can all of these men really be classed as failures?"

Of course not but I can understand the point the secretary makes. Mind you, when I say I agree with much of what Ernie says I don't want anyone talking about me. I don't go along with everything!

Time will tell, of course, whether or not Andy was the right man for the job but, whatever else, he should be given his chance just like others before him. He has plenty of experience — a different kind to being manager of a club — and there are people in every corner of the world who will vouch for his knowledge of the game. When he was SFA Director of Coaching alone and not involved in the national side he was forever being asked to go abroad to demonstrate his coaching skills and to give lectures. Even now he still spends a lot of time out of the country spreading the word.

And the players who have come through the youth team that he was in charge of for so long haven't exactly done badly. Pat Nevin, Paul McStay, Eric Black, John Robertson, Steve Clarke and even Ally McCoist were all given a good grounding in football by the man they now play for at senior level. In addition to all that, he was a coach when I started out at Clydebank so that's something else he's got going in his favour!

Without doubt, his strongest point is his tactical knowledge and his organisational qualities. It was Charlie Nicholas who once said: "Andy has organised a meeting. It's a meeting to tell us when the next meeting is!" He likes the blackboard, of course, and you would expect that from a former teacher but if it helps get a point across there doesn't seem to me to be anything wrong with the idea.

The problem for Andy, and ironically it might be a hangover from his days as youth team boss, is that he's not the type of manager who will scare the players. I don't mean he should frighten them to death but it does take a kind of hard man which he is certainly not. That will not make his job any easier because while it's good that a gaffer can get on with his workers you simply can't get too pally with anyone. It can create problems discipline-wise, although to be fair, I detect quite a change in him since he took over the hot seat.

There are two other individual reasons why Andy will not find it easy to be successful. One is Graeme Souness and the other is Kenny Dalglish. They both opted out of international football recently and that could not have come at a worse time for Andy. Heaven knows, we're not so well off for quality players that we can get by without the likes of Souness and Dalglish. Any manager would have missed players like them. They are irreplaceable simply because both are world class. Imagine Andy's thoughts when they decided enough was enough. He lost his two best players at a stroke and that made an uphill task a veritable mountain to climb. And it would have been the same for any manager. It's just Andy's misfortune that it happened to him.

But, in a broader sense, it's a difficult job anyway. You need bricks and mortar to build a house, not straw. The simple explanation is the same as it was directly after Mexico and the World Cup. We do not have enough quality players. We can talk round the problem for as long as we like and we can delude ourselves as often as we like but the answer stares us straight in the face whether it's the one you want to hear or not.

Sometimes I think that's the greatest difficulty of all. Maybe some people don't want to hear the truth, the whole truth and nothing but the truth. But that's it as I see it and I genuinely don't believe any Scotland manager will ever be totally successful. We might continue to qualify for the World Cup finals and we might even one day do the same for the European Championships. But win them? Not a hope.

Even an amalgam of the four managers I have played for at international level couldn't make something out of next to nothing but if you put their best qualities together it would certainly make an interesting boss.

The only thing I would take from Ally MacLeod is his enthusiasm but that, nevertheless, is vital. From Jock Stein I would take his ability to motivate and his methods of man management. He always seemed to be able to say the right thing at the right time and there's no doubt he knew how to get the very best out of what was at his disposal. From Andy Roxburgh I would gather his tactical knowledge and his classic interest in organising. Maybe Charlie's quote should read: "Let's have a meeting to organise a meeting and then we'll have the real meeting!"

From Fergie I would look for his uncanny ability to read a game but that's only scraping at the surface of the man. It might come as a surprise but he is the pick of the four national bosses I have played under. I have respect for them all for their ways of going about it but to me he is a great manager.

If we could put them altogether, though, all we would need after that is the players!

Chapter Eleven

THE NAME GAME

I T HAS been my pleasure and privilege to play with and against some of the great names in world football ranging from Arbroath to Australia and Motherwell to Mexico. For the most part I have thoroughly enjoyed pitting my wits against them and I would like to think my opponents would say the same thing. But not all the men I admire have been in the opposition ranks. I have been lucky enough also to play alongside top-class players.

Here I would like to indulge myself and list the lads I have had a lot of time for throughout my career. I have come into contact with many — occasionally on the wrong end of a badly aimed size ten boot — and others I have watched from the sidelines. Not all are necessarily superstars — at least not in the recognised manner of the word — but to me they all possess star qualities of some sort and I would like to think it's a catalogue, mainly, of all that's good in this great game.

The venue for my first choice is not one of the great sporting arenas for, let's face it, Kilbowie Park, Clydebank, will never be a Maracana Stadium. But for all that it is a ground that means a lot to me and if one player typified the club where I began my career then it has to be Jim Fallon.

The big centre-half used to be known as Mr Consistency and that tells you something about his attributes. When I arrived at

Clydebank, Jim seemed to have been there for ages and for that matter he seemed to be there for ages after I left as well! But throughout his magnificent service to Bankies he simply got on with the job in hand. Every game, every performance was the same. Nothing varied. He was the epitome of consistency and although he regularly received offers to go elsewhere he stayed at Kilbowie because he enjoyed his football there so much. Recently, of course, he was coaching alongside Sam Henderson at the club before going to Airdrie and any budding professional coming under his wing could do a lot worse than listen to what he's got to say. If they do, they'll not go far wrong.

When I moved to Rangers, naturally I was surrounded by better players and over my decade at Ibrox there have been a host of lads I have rated highly for one reason or another.

In my early days — he won't thank me for saying that — there were few better in this country than Derek Johnstone. He was, without doubt, the best header of a ball I have ever seen. He had the great ability to get up well and somehow hover before powering the ball away with the merest nod of his head. He was a winger's dream to play alongside because he turned bad crosses into good ones and I appreciated that talent more than once. I wouldn't go as far as to say that he made me look good at times but at least I knew that he would make something out of whatever kind of service I provided and it was a comforting thought.

In our treble-winning season of 1977-78 it was DJ who pulled us out of the mire more often than anyone. It was his vital goals that regularly separated Rangers from the others and at the end of a glorious year he had scored 38, which by any standards isn't bad. Yet, strangely, Derek always said he preferred playing in his other role of centre-half where, I'm bound to say, he looked equally at home. He played there on numerous occasions and looked quite comfortable although personally I preferred it when he was up front waiting for a cross from me.

But if he was lethal on the field take it from me he was the same off it where he was always messing about. He was one of the characters that every dressing-room needs although I can't remember saying that when he once cut the sleeves off my shirt.

There was another famous occasion when he incurred the wrath of Sandy Jardine who was very much a senior professional at Ibrox and, for that matter, for Scotland. Sandy used to travel through from Edinburgh and, not surprisingly, he had to do so in all sorts of weather. Eventually, in the depths of one particularly bad winter, he invested in a pair of wellington boots which became a regular sight lying around the dressing-room. These wellies were just too much for DJ to continue ignoring and after a while he had the inspired idea of painting the famous Adidas three stripes on the boots. The rest of the lads loved it but I'm not sure Sandy saw the funny side of it because I don't think the paint ever came off.

It was all fairly harmless, though, and stories about the big man and his exploits are legendary. Above all, however, he was a great Ranger — indeed still is — and people should remember that rather than, as some do, his second spell at Ibrox which wasn't anything like as successful as his glory days there.

Another star of the same era was undoubtedly Tom Forsyth whom many fans identified as a big, hard man. Yet he's a big softie, really!

Not that I ever hazarded that opinion at the time for I spent most of my early years at Ibrox keeping out of his way at training. He was one of these guys who couldn't keep training and playing separate and insisted on approaching both as if his life depended on it. I used to argue with him all the time over at the Albion training ground because he looked at me sometimes as if I had a Celtic jersey on and then acted accordingly. I had to keep reminding him I was on his side.

He's best remembered, probably, for that marvellous tackle on Mick Channon that prevented a certain goal in the 1976 Scotland-England international but really there is so much more to big Tam. He scored that remarkable goal in the 1973 Scottish Cup final victory over Celtic but I don't think he would argue with me — at least I hope he wouldn't! — if I said scoring wasn't exactly his strong point. I remember setting up one goal for him against Dundee when I crossed and he actually stumbled into a header which beat the goalkeeper. I don't know who was most surprised — him, us, the opposition or the crowd — but when it dawned on the fans who had actually notched the goal they went berserk and the look on Tam's face was almost apologetic, as if he shouldn't really have done it.

On another occasion we couldn't believe our eyes when he sold someone a dummy in the middle of a crucial game. He sent the guy the wrong way, brilliantly — almost as if he did it all the time — and then emerged from the move laughing out loud at his own efforts. You couldn't help but laugh as well.

One player who never seemed to laugh much at him, however, was Dundee United's Paul Sturrock who is a smashing player and has had lots of success in a fine career. But he never had much against Tam. "Jaws" — how he hates that nickname — used to put the fear of God into Paul and I can't remember the Tannadice man ever doing well against him.

It was Forsyth's tackling that won him so much praise and rightly so but in a European Cup tie against Cologne he seemed to meet his match. The German lad and Tam clashed in the middle of the park, both went about four feet over the innocent little ball and while it lay gently on the ground minding its own business the two players got on with it. It was fearsome. Funnily enough, the Cologne player didn't play in the return game.

Much as Tam could dish out the stick, though, he could take it as well and he got a nasty thigh knock in a League Cup tie at Arbroath in November 1978. He, Tommy McLean and I were given a lift back to Glasgow after that match at Gayfield and all the way home the wee man and I were winding big Tam up about the "slight" knock he had taken. We never gave him a minute's peace all the way back about how a wee kick had affected the so-called hard man. The next day McLean phoned me and said: "Have you heard about big Tam? He was rushed into hospital in the middle of the night and he'll be in for a few days." It seemed that a serious clot had developed and we felt a bit awful after all the stick we had given him. But he couldn't have been that upset about it. After all, I'm still around to tell the tale!

Another player who was an integral part of that triumphant side was undoubtedly Bobby Russell, who was built like an X-ray but was stronger than many people imagined. Not that strength was his game, rather it was his delicate skill that did so much for Rangers at the time.

Considering he went straight into the team from junior football the impact he made was remarkable. He and I formed an almost telepathic understanding that I have shared with only one other player — Jim Bett. "Rusty" knew exactly what I was doing and vice versa and the partnership worked a treat. It was a delight to have him in the same side and apart from anything else he became my closest friend at Ibrox. Bett came along a bit later but he and I established the same kind of understanding at club and country level. They are two brilliant players.

Around that time, too, we had John McClelland whose influence on the team I have documented elsewhere and Robert Prytz. I don't think the latter got on with John Greig very well either but his biggest problem was that the Premier League just

*The combined efforts of Roy Aitken, Tony Shepherd and Ted McMinn(!)
manage to stop me in my tracks. Trust Ted.*

didn't suit his style of play. It's a pity really because there's no
doubt he is a quality player and he has proved that often enough
since with various clubs and with Sweden for whom he has a
tremendous record at international level.

More recently, there have been plenty of other players whom I
have enjoyed playing alongside and some of the names will be long
remembered for various reasons. Ted McMinn, for example, is
one. Big, daft Ted could be a world-beater one day and the next —
or even later the same day! — he would look as if he had never
been introduced to a football. There's absolutely no doubt they
broke the mould after him.

I can honestly say I have never come across anyone quite like
him because at his best he was absolutely brilliant and at his worst,
well, he was appalling. He scored a goal against Dumbarton straight
from a corner once and his celebration jog took him halfway round
the pitch before ending back where he had started. Nothing
daunted, Ted waltzed around the corner flag for a few seconds and
it was the funniest thing I've seen. Mind you, Terry Butcher always
reckoned his funniest memory in football was meeting Ted for the

Ally McCoist and I are just good pals . . . honest.

first time. I can understand that but he's a great lad.

The supporters loved him too and he seemed to get a special cheer whatever he did. He fell over his own feet in a game at Ibrox and they cheered and applauded him as if he had scored the winning goal in the European Cup final. There has to be room for entertainers like that. There was never a dull moment when he was around, that's for sure.

The same can be said for Ally McCoist, the dressing-room clown who occasionally borders on lunacy! He's a great guy to have there, though, because he's the same all the time, a flamboyant character who tries hard not to let anything get him down and if he wasn't a footballer then I reckon he would have been a singer. He does a "rap" song that is nothing short of sensational and it's a party piece he has perfected through the years of doing it in a variety of places. He'll stand up and belt out the rap on a coach or in a restaurant and on a trip I missed, I later heard about Chelsea officials being utterly amazed, and impressed, when he did just that in a plush London eating-place after a friendly at Stamford Bridge a few years ago.

Ally can play football into the bargain. He has come through a period when he got some stick from supporters but he answered all the critics by doing what he does best — scoring goals — and had the last laugh. But that's the great thing about him. You're never too far away from a laugh when he's around and he's worth his weight in gold — or is it goals?

There were many fine aspects about Rangers in last season's tremendous campaign and it's difficult to see past the English influence when we talk success stories. If you had told me a couple of years ago that I would be playing alongside the likes of Chris Woods, Terry Butcher and Graham Roberts at Ibrox I would have called for the men in white coats to come and take you away. Yet they arrived at Ibrox at different times and joined forces in a triangle that is the backbone of just about every successful side in the history of the game, goalkeeper and central defenders. Get that right and you're a long way towards doing well in football.

When you talk about 'keepers — wherever they are in the world — you tend to think about any flaws they have. The trouble with Chris is that he hasn't got any! He is one of the most significant reasons behind the Rangers revival. He is good in the air, has terrific positional sense and seems to dominate the goal. I kid him on that he's about ninth in line to be England's number one but there's no doubt that he's already there in reality. He's a quiet lad

Ally and I keep a firm grip on the League Cup.

but I have worked out why. It's only because he's speechless at the number of goals Ally McCoist and I knock past him in training every day.

In front of him, Terry Butcher is quite simply the best defender I've ever seen. In fact he is the defence. He could be a back four on his own he's so good. Tel just doesn't seem to have a weakness. He's got a great touch for a big man, he is virtually unbeatable in the air and he can play great passes out of defence to the front men. The opposition must look at Terry and wonder how on earth they're going to get the better of him. Hopefully, they won't work it out for a long time. He is also club captain, of course, and it's impossible to think of anyone better equipped for the job. He has the respect of all the lads, is vastly experienced and is a magnificent ambassador for Rangers on and off the field. The same could be said for his efforts for England but since I spend half my life giving "Lurch" stick about his nationality I'll not dwell on what a good job

127

he does for them. We have a constant running battle about the Scotland-England thing and we're forever striking bets when the two countries meet in any kind of sport. It gets boring, though, continually taking money off him!

The last part of the triangle is Graham Roberts and, like Terry and Chris, he'll get over the fact that he's English. More seriously, I felt a bit sorry for Graham last season for it was obvious his reputation for being a bit of a hard man down south had preceded him when he came to Ibrox. He used to get in a bit of trouble occasionally when he played in England but as far as I'm concerned it is his natural enthusiasm and exuberance that has caused problems and certainly not any malice or ill-will. Anyway, he's a tremendous guy to have on your side and a rock in the heart of the defence. Mind you, he's not a bad goalkeeper either and if the 'keepers are having specialist training at any time he's the first to go between the posts. I'm fed up with his story of how he once went in goal for Tottenham in a European tie and kept a clean sheet!

Our success, though, isn't just about Englishmen for in Irishman Jimmy Nicholl we have a tremendous professional. I was delighted when he came back to Rangers for a second spell and he's doing as well as ever.

But there has been a huge home influence on the side as well and if I pick out two youngters in the squad I hope the others, all of whom play a part, will bear with me. Ian Durrant is going to be a world-class player if he progresses as he should. It's one of his superstitions that he always runs out of the tunnel after me but it's his runs on the pitch that I appreciate more. He is a marvellously unselfish player and takes up great position whether or not he gets the ball. One time he did was when I released a pass to him in last season's opening Old Firm game and he showed a maturity far beyond his years with the manner in which he took the goal. I have every confidence that he'll go on to great things.

His "partner" is Derek Ferguson and really when you look at the pair of them there's no limit to what they can achieve if they stick at it. They are two very different players but both are exceptional for their age. Derek is more a touch player than Ian and doesn't have his pal's eye for a goal but he's got almost unbelievable skill and will, I'm sure, do just as well.

Last, but not least or he'll make my life a misery, is the gaffer. Graeme Souness is a world-class player, as I have said elsewhere in this book, and he has been sorely missed at international level. But

All wrapped up before the Skol Cup Final . . . and the trophy was wrapped up later!

we're fortunate he has kept on doing it for Rangers despite the extra burden of being boss and that has proved beneficial for *every* player at Ibrox. Graeme has the kind of arrogance associated with the old-time gunslingers and I think it's fair to say that there are players in the world genuinely scared of him. He has a remarkable talent aided and abetted by an ability to take care of himself. Not many players can combine the two but he does very effectively. Few players do him for skill and equally few succeed in taking him on physically. He'll always be a target because there are always guys who want to prove — just like the old Wild West — that they are better but he's used to that. And at the end of it all he has been inspirational on the field for us despite a couple of well-publicised incidents last season.

There have been other players over my years at Ibrox who have influenced me one way or the other but this list contains the names I feel have been that bit special. Similarly, I have come across opponents of all shapes and sizes and at almost every club there are, or have been, players I have admired. This book would need to be the size of *War and Peace*, however, to give them all their place. Instead, I'll select a random few again and I have already made mention of the respect I have for Danny McGrain and Roy Aitken and what they have done, and in Roy's case are still doing, for Celtic.

They have shown tremendous loyalty to their club and the same can be said for Willie Miller of Aberdeen. He is a terrific player who has an enviable record of consistency for both Dons and Scotland. You can always rely on Willie to be there when you most need him and while I have always admired that when he's in a Scotland jersey there are times when I could have done without it at club level. He is the lynchpin of the all-important defensive triangle I talked about earlier, alongside Alex McLeish in front of Jim Leighton. Willie, in addition, is as good a referee as I have ever seen or heard. First of all he is a terrible moaner when a decision goes against him and after that he complains non-stop. When he finishes playing, and if he doesn't become a coach or a manager, then he could be a ref — he would even be given a whistle then.

Another Aberdeen star who impresses me is full-back Stewart McKimmie who I reckon is a very good player. I always find him a difficult opponent and he's a helluva man for making forward runs all the time. He's a bit like Danny McGrain in that respect and I curse them both for it when I have to check back every couple of minutes.

I'm doing it here but manager Graeme Souness keeps on doing it for Rangers and he's never usually in the background.

One other lad on the domestic front who seems to reserve his best games for when he comes across Rangers is Alan Rough. The Hibs 'keeper just seems to stand in the middle of his goal and become a magnet for the ball when we play them. He seems to be able to stop everything we throw at him. Against that, however, I have seen "Scruff" make a few mistakes in his time. There's no in-between with him. He's either brilliant — invariably against us — or he can be the opposite.

So much for domestic club level. But what about the Scotland scene? Obviously there have been lots of very good players in the international teams I have played in but probably only two really stand out. One is the afore-mentioned Souness and the other, of course, is Kenny Dalglish who was an absolute joy to play alongside. They don't come along like Kenny too often and I'm glad I can say I played in the same team as him a few times.

He was a maestro — or maybe that should be a Rolls Royce! — of a player who seemed to know instinctively exactly what to do with the ball for the best. It irritated me a bit when some folk would look at his international record and say: "He's got all those caps but he's only really played well in a handful of matches." If that was the case then just about every good judge of football has been wrong over the years.

He would be the first name down on any team sheet of mine and, come to that, he was when I set about naming a side consisting only of players I have played with at club and international level. It was an interesting exercise and there's no doubt I was spoilt for choice but here's my final eleven, in 4-3-3 formation, with a couple of substitutes thrown in for good measure: Chris Woods, Jimmy Nicholl, Tom Forsyth, Terry Butcher, John Greig, Bobby Russell, Graeme Souness, Jim Bett, Kenny Dalglish, Derek Johnstone, Davie Cooper. I took the liberty of including myself! My substitutes would be Ian Durrant and Willie Miller.

All sorts of quality players are missing from there but as I see it that wouldn't be a bad team and I, for one, wouldn't have minded appearing in it when all the guys were at their peak. There is safety and power at the back, subtlety and steel in the middle of the park and flair and plenty of goals available up front.

But while all these many and varied players are tremendously gifted professionals I have to say I think, with the odd exception, we step up in class when we move into the European and global areas. I have played against, and watched, any number of foreign stars and generally they are more talented or, if you prefer it, have more basic skills than most of the lads produced in Britain.

Once again, I have looked back through the years and it wasn't difficult to pick_out a selection of players I would pay to go and watch myself. The list begins in my first season with Rangers when we met the Dutch Cup holders Twente. Basically we were murdered by them in Holland yet ironically two players who later came to these shores and did tremendously well impressed me most of all. Arnold Muhren played for Ipswich Town and Manchester United here and just last season won a European Cup Winners Cup medal with Ajax, when that brilliant left foot looked just as good then as it did a decade ago. His partner in the Twente team, though, was Frans Thijssen who also went to Portman Road and was part of a terrific side which included our own Terry Butcher. They gave me my first serious lessons in the continental way of playing the game but there have been plenty of others since.

The following year we stumbled into Juventus and actually beat them. I didn't play in either game but watching from the sidelines gave me a fair insight into the quality of their players. Tardelli, Cabrini, Causio etc. They were all there — nine of the Italian World Cup team — but the one who impressed me most was Roberto Bettega. Even in that company I thought he stood out.

In the next round of that year's European Cup we played West Germany or, rather, the Cologne side who had a fair sprinkling of international players on view as well. Top of the list — at least I'm sure he would like to believe that — was the arrogant goalkeeper Harald Schumacher who made it look as if no one should ever have the affrontery to score against him. Then there was Cullmann, Schuster, Littbarski and the one I liked best, Flohe.

The following year we met up with Germans again in the shape of Fortuna Dusseldorf and the man who caught my eye there was undoubtedly Klaus Allofs. He and his brother Thomas were both in the opposition and although Klaus wasn't very well known at that time I saw the potential and he went on to become an excellent player.

Our European opponents seemed to read like a *Who's Who* of football at that time for next in line were Valencia who boasted the impressive Mario Kempes and Rainer Bonhof. The Argentinian star destroyed us with the pace and technique he had shown in helping his country to the 1978 World Cup victory and about the only "fault" I could find with him was that he needed a haircut!

The next hit-man to make his mark on me was Fernando Gomes of FC Porto whose goal in Portugal knocked us out of the Cup

Winners Cup in 1983-84. It wasn't one of the greatest goals in the history of the competition but it amply illustrated that he was a great striker with the happy knack of being in exactly the right place at exactly the right time.

Alessandro Altobelli, Liam Brady, Guiseppe Bergomi and Karl-Heinz Rummenigge spelled Inter Milan and trouble the following year although we were very unlucky to go out. All those players had the special stamp of class on them.

If there was any one place, however, when I could see close up the difference in class between British players and foreign ones then it was the World Cup finals in Mexico in 1986. In our opening game we came up against a succession of tremendous players for Denmark like Morten Olsen, Soren Lerby, Frank Arnesen, Preban Elkjaer and the finest of them all, Michael Laudrup. The latter has to be one of the greatest players in the world right now. Then West Germany had all the familiar names but it was Hans-Peter Briegel I rated above them all. If I hadn't been playing for a brief few minutes I would have been happy to admire him.

But when you looked at the World Cup squads from the various countries most seemed to have maybe eight or nine players you could genuinely call world class. Belgium had Jean-Marie Pfaff, Eric Gerets, Franky Van der Elst, Franky Vercautern, Rene Vandereycken, Enzo Scifo and Jan Ceulemans among others. Brazil had Josimar, Edinho, Junior, Socrates, Falcao, Zico and Casagrande while la belle France, that fabulous side, had Manuel Amoros, Patrick Battiston, Maxime Bossis, Bernard Genghini, Alain Giresse, Michel Platini, Jean Tigana and Yannick Stopyra. For Spain there was Zubizarreta, Maceda, Gallego, Victor, Caldere, Rincon, Butragueno and Carrasco. And the Russians could call on Rinat Dasayev, Vladimir Bessonov, Alexander Chivadze, Antoly Demyanenko, Vassil Rats and Igor Belanov.

It's a galaxy of names and up till now I haven't even mentioned the greatest of them all, Diego Maradona of Argentina. He always amazes me because of his build. He's got fantastic pace for basically a wee guy and, really, he appears to have absolutely everything.

If I'm waxing a bit lyrical about all these foreigners then don't sit holding your breath waiting for an apology. I admire quality players, players with above average skill and talent and players who can excite and entertain. Believe me, I would like nothing better than to have a handful of Scots — or even British — players I could put into that exalted company. But with my hand on my heart I just can't do it and there's no doubt in my mind why. We are beaten by the system.

Chapter Twelve

OLD PROBLEMS
AND A NEW ERA

THE Premier League does absolutely nothing to encourage players with above-average skill and ability and I for one have never found it suits my style of play. Indeed, I have only stayed in the division and the country because of my reluctance to leave my family. If the choice had been only about football and nothing else then, believe me, I would have been up, up and away and taking advantage of the offers from elsewhere I have had fairly regularly throughout my career.

To be brutally frank, the Premier League is the last place I would advise players of real talent to pursue their careers, for it's very seldom they are given a reasonable chance to actually play and I must say I find that a bit sad. After all, the game is meant to be about entertainment but our entertainment is different from anywhere else.

It's not just coincidence, you know, that the world-class men all play abroad. Not too many of them would survive in our league where there are as many hammer-throwers as there are players. Basically, the Premier League kills class. Any decent player gets his ability kicked out of him whereas in Europe you are given more time on the ball and therefore there is a greater chance of the finer points of the game flourishing. Not so here where a fair number of our matches are like the games we had at school when it was 32-a-

The Premier League is a tough place to earn a living.

side and everyone charged about like headless chickens. Not only that, they are really tall headless chickens and I sometimes wonder if a lot of our players are only in the game because they are over six feet tall. Height and strength seem to be the right qualifications whereas skill and ability are almost secondary in many places. Some of these guys would kick their grandmothers and it's difficult, with the best will in the world and the greatest imagination, to see how Diego Maradona or Michael Laudrup would survive.

137

It all leaves me a bit frustrated and I'm sure there are other players in the country who feel the same way. The fact that we aren't allowed to play as much as we would like doesn't mean very much on its own but put that factor into the general scheme of things and it's easy to see why genuine world-class players are few and far between here. We get the occasional top-class player but it's about as regular as a sighting of Haley's Comet and it's no wonder we struggle to field exceptional players in the Scotland squad. We can never be an international force as long as the system dictates that stamina is more important than skill, tension replaces talent and kickers are rewarded in the same way as class players.

Part of the problem, to me, is the fact that we have so many games and that meeting every other club a minimum of four times a season does nothing other than make familiarity breed contempt. Feuds are carried over game to game and when that happens there's even less chance of having a constructive 90 minutes.

But there is another aspect to it all and while it might not mean a lot to some people it does to me. The problem is that so many of our grounds and pitches are so poor. I am a winger but sometimes there are no wings. Take Hamilton's Douglas Park, for example. If I was to stand on the wing there I would be in the fast lane of the M74. It's probably a bit unfair to knock clubs like that because they have such limited resources but it's places like Douglas Park where the ball tends to be in the air so much it gets a headache.

Youngsters can't develop properly when that's happening and that can't in turn be good for the game. I tend to think that you will find out whether a player can play or not at places like Ibrox or Dens Park where there is room to express yourself. I'm not sure, for instance, if youngsters like Ian Durrant and Derek Ferguson would have come on so well if they had been elsewhere.

Altogether it's not a pretty picture and it leaves us trailing miles behind Europe and the rest of the world. I can't see it ever changing either. The Premier League will continue to be packed with average players and that in turn means we will always have an international team that struggles in amongst real quality.

It would be nice to think otherwise and maybe if the fans could accept changes away from kick-and-rush football then we could make progress accordingly. Supporters tend to like blood and thunder and thud and blunder but that way is quickly found out in the rarified atmosphere of the World Cup finals.

It really does get to me at times and, without making excuses for myself, it's my frustration over the years that has led me into so

Fall guy. This time it's Celtic's Derek Whyte who sends me flying.

many bookings. I would estimate that 95 per cent of my misdemeanours are for chirping. The other five per cent are for getting in the road, because no one could ever accuse me of kicking!

But maybe some of these cautions could have been avoided, too, with the help of others. It's always been my opinion, only an opinion, that referees should have played the game at senior level. That way they would know exactly what was going on, they would appreciate more the things that happen and maybe, just maybe, they would realise why.

139

That would be my first improvement if I had any say whatsoever in the game. And my second would be to pay them better. They get a paltry sum for spending their Saturday afternoons or Wednesday nights getting roundly abused by all and sundry. They are needed in the game so why should they not be rewarded accordingly? I'll tell you here and now I wouldn't do their job for the kind of money they get at the moment. Mind you, I don't really think I would be cut out for the job anyway!

Obviously there are a great many around the country and around the world who know how to go about it and I reckon generally they have the same characteristics that appeal to players. For a start, you can talk to them and make a valid point without having a yellow card waved in front of your face the minute you open your mouth. They'll simply tell you to get on with it and even manage to share a laugh at times. They're confident with it and when players see that they respect officials for it.

Sadly, though, I'm sure everyone realises there are exceptions to the rule as in other areas. That's particularly so when an official will make a production of calling you from over 30 yards away to tell you you're a naughty boy. It's like being an errant schoolboy up before the teacher. Talk about making a drama out of a crisis! But I don't want to be critical — I might get another red card! — and instead let me emphasise that I believe the standard is good overall.

The biggest problem and no-one will ever find a cure for this is that referees are only human. It's as easy for them to make mistakes as it is for players — and as fans are quick to remind us we make plenty! — and all I would say is that maybe there is a way to accommodate better referees as well as better players but it will need a louder voice than mine to start that particular ball rolling.

But if that's a revolution which might have to wait awhile another is well under way in Scotland. This particular revolution started way back on 7 April 1986 when Jock Wallace left Rangers and was instantly replaced by Graeme Souness. To say it was a shock to the world of football would be to say the first man on the moon just went out for an evening stroll.

It was, in short, a sensation. Big Jock had won two League Cups since his return but that is never enough at Ibrox. The Championship is what matters most and, in fairness, we didn't look ready to make any kind of bid for that. Instead, we had struggled through the winter and when spring appeared we were doing little other than play out time in another disappointing season. Rangers

I have to be honest . . . this is not an unusual photograph.

clearly felt that was not good enough and when a club makes that kind of decision there is only one possible outcome.

So the manager went and I have to say I was desperately sorry about that. Big Jock and I had a tremendous relationship during both his spells at Ibrox and I owe him an awful lot. He was good for me.

As the club was announcing his departure, Jock was holding an emotional press conference at Glasgow's Grosvenor Hotel and the drama, like a soap opera, was unfolding minute by minute. Yet the first I knew of it all was when my wife Christine shouted up the stairs at our Motherwell home. I was lying in the bath and when she said Graeme Souness was the new manager of Rangers I damn nearly drowned in surprise! The news was harder to digest than the bath water but when it sunk in — if you'll pardon the expression — my initial reactions were probably not what you would expect.

I was pessimistic and concerned. That might sound strange in view of the excitement and euphoria that followed the announcement but I was only concerned about myself. Number one. I have never been what you would call a grafter and I wasn't sure what the new boss would make of that. Sure, I do all the training and, hopefully, pay my way when the serious action starts but I'm the first to admit I don't relish extra work. I also briefly believed that Graeme would want to bring in youngsters immediately and that too would have threatened my place at Ibrox.

I know I wasn't alone with these thoughts for when a new manager comes in to a club every player has to take a long, hard look at himself and try and work out what the future will hold. Everyone is a little apprehensive, wondering exactly where they would stand with the incoming gaffer. It's at times like that I look to my family and friends for reassurance and together with what they say and I know I eventually sort things out.

So, almost as quickly as those thoughts entered my head they were dismissed and replaced with my old self-belief which has carried me through all my career. I reasoned, rightly or wrongly, that I have ability and why should a new manager want to do away with that? I also thought, after the initial misgivings, that this really could be the start of something big for Rangers Football Club.

I was enthusiastic therefore when I sat in the dressing-room with all the other players awaiting the arrival of Graeme and looking forward to hearing what he had to say. The dressing-room, mind you, was very quiet as the players sat with their own thoughts. Some, clearly, were at ease with the prospect while others were edgy and I can understand that. It really was a step into the unknown.

But it was exactly the same for Graeme and he admitted as much

I've got time on my hands while Dundee United's Iain Ferguson has something a good deal prettier. We're celebrating individual Skol Cup success.

in that first dressing-room chat. He came in and started by saying: "This is hard for me because I don't know many of you. But right now the only thing you need to concern yourselves with is getting this club in European football next season."

That, in essence, was it because he had to fly back to Italy where he was still under contract to Sampdoria and he didn't have a lot of time to get to know his new staff. But the message he gave us was simple and straightforward. We had struggled to the point where missing out on a Euro place was a distinct possibility and he knew that was absolutely no use to a club the size and stature of Rangers. I got the impression he didn't fancy missing out himself either so we were under no illusions about that.

It all left the youngsters open-mouthed and the senior players not far behind. It was a remarkable sight to see Graeme Souness in

143

the Ibrox dressing-room but even more astonishing to listen to him
as the new manager of Rangers.

The mood when he was gone was positive and that became even
more clear when, a week or so later, it was announced that Walter
Smith, assistant manager to Jim McLean at Dundee United, was
taking over as number two to Graeme. Wattie had an outstanding
track record at Tannadice where he and Jim had worked a regular
miracle. And in fairness to the United manager he was always
quick to give credit where credit was due as far as Wattie was
concerned. So we knew roughly just what an acquisition he would
be to Rangers and early impressions merely confirmed that. He got
everything so well organised and while he got on well with
everyone we all realised that he was no soft touch. Now I know him
better I give him stick all day long and moan constantly. Eventually
it gets to him and just as he's about to take a kick at me in training
I'll remind him: "I'm a player and you can't kick us." Even at that
time it looked an inspired signing, though, for Walter knows
everything there is to know about Scottish football — on the
manager's own admission not his strong point after years down
south and in Italy — and he looked an ideal partner for the boss.

He, I'm sure, knew exactly where we were struggling and for
that matter it wouldn't have needed a coaching genius to realise
that the first thing we had to do if we wanted to qualify for Europe
was tighten up in defence. We simply couldn't keep on letting in
goals the way we had been and a classic example of that failing had
come just a couple of weeks before Graeme's appointment when
we had drawn 4-4 with Celtic. Imagine scoring four goals in an Old
Firm match and not winning. That's a disgrace. So the defence
always had to be a priority and that's how it eventually worked out
with the signings of Messrs. Woods, Butcher and Roberts.

From the start the players knew they were playing not only for a
European future but for their own futures. Careers were at stake
and there was never a better illustration of that than one day when
Graeme was making a flying visit back to this country from Genoa.
He ordered a full-scale training match on the pitch at Ibrox and
right away that was a bit different for most days we did our work
over at the Albion training ground.

So the stage was set and it was more like a cup final than a
training stint. The lads were only too well aware that they were on
trial and the judge and jury were sitting in the Directors' Box in the
shape of Graeme and Walter. It was very tense and very nerve-
racking, for the players realised that the guy who could make or

New Rangers manager . . . Graeme Souness.

break them was scrutinising every move, every pass and every tackle. I've actually never known a training game like it. Players were getting whacked and there was a bit of needle to it all as people tried to create a favourable impression. It's amazing the effect a new manager has!

But at least it had the desired effect for the team got its act together in time and we qualified for Europe by beating Motherwell 2-0 at Ibrox on the last day of the season. It's just as well we did, for while there were always going to be drastic changes I believe there would have been far more had we missed out on that money-spinning spot.

There was a fantastic atmosphere in the ground, though, and a definite expectation that the club was going places . . . and not just into Europe! Some players were going places, too. I suspect the players who left knew themselves they would be going. Derek Johnstone, Dave McKinnon, Eric Ferguson, Billy Davies and Andy Bruce were among those making early exits.

At the same time, though, we got an idea of how high the manager was aiming when he made a bid to take Richard Gough from Dundee United. It failed because the Tannadice team wouldn't sell the defender to another Scottish club but it certainly set the trend. It had the place buzzing and the newspapers were rife with speculation about who Graeme would go for next. So were the players for that matter because we liked to take a passing interest in what is going on as well.

The first big-money arrival at Ibrox was striker Colin West from Watford but no one was under any illusions that he would be the last newcomer. The wheeling and dealing, though, was interrupted a little by the small matter of the World Cup finals in Mexico and the gaffer, Wattie and I were all in the party that left Scotland.

In some ways, I suppose, the other two could have done without the tournament because it seemed they had enough on their plates thinking about Ibrox and what the next moves would be. So it was long-distance transfer activity and I gather the newspapers back home produced a kind of who's who of world football as Rangers' targets. One name I heard mentioned at our training camp was Roberto Falcao but in the end I was intrigued to learn that the man in question was Norwich City and England 'keeper Chris Woods. Any lingering doubts I might have had about the club's ambitions went at that point for as his country's number two 'keeper Chris was obviously a big name. And there was a certain irony for me that, after years of refusing to go south, here I was being joined by

I'm not sure where I'm going after the managerial switch.

Englishmen back in my own country! It was certainly a departure from the usual trail of players crossing the border in a southerly direction but judging by the stir it caused it was also more than welcome.

All this manoeuvring, though, was brought to a halt by the manager himself as the World Cup games drew ever closer and instead he devoted himself, as did Walter, 100 per cent to the Scotland cause. He was not, however, above having the occasional chat with me about Rangers. I wouldn't for a second suggest he ever took me into his confidence regarding players or anything like that because clearly it would have been wrong to do so but there were other aspects of the club that he was interested in hearing about.

I did my best to fill in the blanks because Ibrox isn't just any football ground in the same way as Rangers isn't just any football club and although Graeme had a wealth of experience from his travels to Tottenham, Middlesbrough, Liverpool and Sampdoria, Glasgow was a bit different.

He listened intently as I outlined the supporters' expectations, gave him an idea of the atmosphere of the place and hopefully pointed him in a few other directions and I must say I was listening just as closely when he let me in on a few plans of his own. There was nothing specific but enough to whet my appetite. There we were enthusing about the possibilities for the following season when the current one was still on the go!

It was my first real get-to-know-you session with the boss and I couldn't really have failed to be impressed. Incidentally, I would say that even if he hadn't agreed to do the foreword to this book! I knew right away that many of his thoughts on the game had emanated from his time at Anfield and to be honest I couldn't see too much wrong with that when I considered his success rate on Merseyside. He won everything there was to win and played under some of the shrewdest judges in the game, so I reasoned he must have known something about it! But he also hinted that one or two Italian-type features would be brought into operation and altogether it sounded a more than interesting prospect.

All the scheming, however, had to be put on ice while we got on with the business in hand and unfortunately, as I have outlined elsewhere, Mexico wasn't the happiest of summer hunting grounds. But despite that and the fact that my summer holidays had been somewhat restricted I could hardly wait for season 1986-87 to begin and while I had a few extra days off because of my

Billy Davies (number 12) is happy enough here but he left soon after Graeme Souness arrived.

international involvement pre-season training couldn't come quick enough . . . even for me.

Graeme, in fact, was at his desk on 7 July and that really was the official start of the Rangers revolution. He had already caused more than a few ripples in Scottish football merely by his own signing and then the other transfers he had been involved with. But those ripples turned into tidal waves not long after and, really, for the 11 months that followed no one at Ibrox had time to catch their breath as we moved from one incident to another in what I think you could safely call an action-packed season.

Chapter Thirteen

A STEP BY STEP
GUIDE TO SUCCESS

FABULOUS, unbelievable, fantastic, magnificent, unforgettable . . . take your pick and even then none of these adjectives adequately sums up season 1986-87 for Rangers Football Club. Just about every conceivable high and low, every peak and every trough were packed into a domestic and European programme that captured headlines the world over and left the Ibrox club the name on everyone's lips. Mind you, in the cool light of day it's easy to see why when you consider the goings-on in and around Govan.

It really began that day when manager Graeme Souness returned to the club for the start of the new season. He was at his desk by 8 a.m. and that maybe gives some idea of how enthusiastic and determined to get on with it the gaffer was.

Ironically, my own season didn't start until a week later for the manager had given me an extra seven days' holiday to get over the World Cup and I was grateful for that. Yet I wasn't bothered that I would be left at the starting gate as far as fitness was concerned because at that point I probably felt better than at any other time in my career. The altitude training in Mexico and a few runs round Strathclyde Park near my Motherwell home ensured I was in good nick and certainly I feel I was as ready for the challenge ahead as anyone else. That's just as well, too, for when I did report back to

Ibrox the rest of the lads were quick to tell me they had been hammered in that first week and I couldn't have afforded to be in bad shape.

Most of the early work was done either at our own Albion training ground across the road from Ibrox or at Jordanhill which also has good facilities. The training, our first pre-season sessions under Graeme and Walter Smith, surprised me initially and it was clear from the outset that the manager was making this part of life the Italian job.

He was very keen to make sure we warmed up for a long time and it wasn't unusual for at least 30 minutes to be spent just on that. He utilised different stretching exercises and it was all designed to avoid the usual pulls and strains footballers get when they go back to work after a lengthy spell of relative inactivity. And as far as I was concerned it seemed to work a treat. It was different and imaginative and although I wouldn't go quite as far as saying I enjoyed it it certainly wasn't the chore it had been to me personally sometimes in the past.

It was a strange time, too, for the lads had to feel their way a bit just as, I suppose, Graeme had to as well. We had to determine the level of patter we could use during sessions and it was a gradual learning process with a new boss and assistant. But for all that it went very smoothly with no real dramas other than occasional transfer talk among us, principally about the club being linked with Ipswich Town and England centre-half Terry Butcher. We already had a shock to the system with the arrival of the likes of Colin West and Chris Woods but, quite honestly, I didn't believe for a second that Rangers could attract Butcher to the Premier League. The idea seemed inconceivable to me at least.

But all thoughts of that were brushed aside when we turned our attentions to a tour of Germany. I'm all in favour of trips like that and it was especially important this time as a getting-to-know-you exercise for all concerned. The squad that left Glasgow — the pool was the first indication of the manager's thoughts — was: Chris Woods, Nicky Walker, Ally Dawson, Hugh Burns, Stuart Munro, Craig Paterson, Dave McPherson, Avi Cohen (who was with us for a trial period), Cammy Fraser, Bobby Russell, Ian Durrant, Derek Ferguson, Ted McMinn, Ally McCoist, Bobby Williamson, Colin West and me. A total of 16 players plus, of course, one other in the shape of the manager. The party was completed by assistant Wattie Smith, physiotherapist Bob Findlay and just one pressman, *Evening Times* sportswriter and co-author of this book, Graham Clark.

Smart but casual . . . the car, not me!

After a brief stop-over in London we headed straight to a tiny little village called Norheim in the Nahe region of south-west Germany and booked into the Sportshotel Bergamo where Walter Smith had stayed previously when he was with Dundee United. The hotel was ideal for there were no distractions but, equally, there was a swimming pool, table-tennis, sauna, solarium and just about everything we could want. The whole place was geared up for visitors just like us and the staff were very friendly.

Not that we had too much time to ourselves for the management pair planned double training sessions at nearby Bad Kreuznach which we reached courtesy of two mini-buses driven Nigel Mansell-like by the gaffer and my co-author. That was enough to bring the lads out in a sweat without the actual training but we survived a few days of it before our first match against SG Union Solingen. What I'm not entirely sure of, though, is how Wattie Smith survived, for the Ibrox number two had a recurring nightmare with the travel arrangements. We got a coach to the game and despite Wattie's assurances that it was "only half an hour away" we were still looking at the German countryside a couple of hours later. He took a fair bit of stick for that.

The 90 minutes' action was fairly uneventful but pretty satisfying and the signs of the way the manager expected us to play were already evident. Basically, the game like the rest of the tour was all about fitness and his pre-match instructions were to give it a blast and if you tired later on there were substitutes available. He never once suggested that results at this stage were the be-all and end-all and while a 2-0 victory — Ally McCoist scored both goals — might not have seemed that inspiring to the folks back home the game served its purpose.

The spirit in the party was great and there were a lot of laughs in between the serious action. We had a tennis tournament at a magnificent complex nearby one night, for example, and although the likes of McCoist and his partner Colin West fancied their chances they would have been as well playing tiddlywinks. They talked a better game than they played and instead it was left to the "experts" — Chris Woods and Nicky Walker against Bobby Russell and myself — to contest the final. There was a fair bit of barracking from Messrs. McCoist and West during the decider but in the end I'm sure they appreciated class and style when Bobby and I won 6-4!

What they, and the rest of us, didn't appreciate however was the lengthy bus trip to our next match against TSV Battenberg. Poor

Wattie got another hammering, although by now he was insisting that it was the manager's organisation and not his. It didn't save him, though, for the managerial alliance cracked when the gaffer disclaimed any knowledge of the travel details.

We drew 1-1 eventually thanks to a West goal from my cross and I must say it immediately brought back to me memories of Derek Johnstone. It was just the kind of goal we had worked between us so often. But, generally, we were quite pleased with our second outing.

At that stage it was beginning to dawn on me that we could be set fair for a good season. The manager's professionalism shone through everything else. He would share a laugh and a joke but when the action got under way nothing stood in the way of us getting fit. The vibes were good.

And they were even better when we dumped Cammy Fraser out of the mini-bus on the way back from training one day! It was the midfield man's birthday and the lads couldn't think of a nicer present than a long walk back to the hotel. Credit where credit's due, though, and Cammy produced a couple of bottles of champagne on the way home from game three later that day. A Dave McPherson tap-in gave us a win in that one against Wurzburg Heidingsfeld and we later suffered our only defeat against Cologne at Koblenz where the local club staged the fixture as part of their 75th anniversary celebrations.

It was a smashing tour on and off the field and if ever a solid base for future success was laid it was there in Germany. The manager and Wattie ensured everything — perhaps except the coach trips! — was just right and while we worked very hard in training and in games there were some memorable moments.

The gaffer, for instance, liked to break the monotony by taking the lads away to somewhere a bit different for dinner and there's no doubt it was a good idea. The only problem was getting to some of the restaurants he chose and coming back again. One never-to-be-forgotten scene involved a mini-bus full of the lads who seemed to be trailing miles behind the coach driven by the boss as we picked our way through a wood. It was only when we got back to the hotel that it transpired *Times* reporter Graham Clark had been driving most of the way with a towel wrapped round his eyes!

That same journey was memorable for a "fight" on board. Things got a bit boisterous — never nasty — and there were bodies everywhere. Cammy Fraser actually emerged with a cut lip and a split eye and I'm not sure what the boss made of it all.

We had another good night at a barbecue at the home of Bernd Killat, the agent who had helped organise the trip. We played a few daft games to pass the time and it was a great break from the more mundane parts of the ten days away. It all broke up the routine a bit and boosted team spirit.

So it was a happy squad who made their way home, boosted still further by the news we heard that Rangers had agreed terms with Ipswich for Butcher's transfer. There was still some way to go, as I knew, before he became a team-mate but it was certainly an interesting thought and when he joined us for a training session back in Glasgow the whole deal seemed to be progressing towards a highly satisfactory conclusion. So it proved and I have to say I was absolutely flabbergasted when Terry signed. Delighted as well of course.

The first time the rest of us saw the big man properly was when he came to watch our friendly against Tottenham at White Hart Lane. He had already signed but I think the club wanted to "unwrap" him at the glamour challenge match against Bayern Munich at our own Ibrox. The 1-1 draw against Spurs was followed by a 2-0 defeat against the German champions but in both matches our supporters saw a new Rangers. It was a side with the emphasis firmly on football and the signs were that we were eminently capable of doing well in the season ahead.

The gaffer himself was, or at least seemed, reasonably satisfied with the progress. Eventually he wanted us to be like his old beloved Liverpool or, for that matter, Bayern Munich. But at the same time he knew that wouldn't come overnight. Generally, however, we were on the right lines and the only blot on my personal horizon was missing the start of the season proper through suspension. With that in mind, indeed, I was taken off in the game against the Germans. So when we got down to the nitty-gritty I was left sitting in the Easter Road stand with my pal Ricky Jordan. Maybe, as things turned out, that was just as well.

The build-up to Rangers' first Premier League match of the season against Hibs was unbelievable. Everyone in the country, it appeared, was talking about Rangers' new players and the new manager and while some — maybe even most — wanted us to do well there were an awful lot of people just waiting and hoping we would fall flat on our faces.

And that, in fact, is exactly what we did. We wanted a good start so much and we were so wound up to get it that we were over-anxious. Games against Hibs are always a bit nervy because I don't think there is much love lost between the two camps so there is always a danger of a flare-up. But Easter Road provided the flare-up to end all flare-ups with manager Graeme Souness right in the middle. The gaffer was sent off, 20 others were later booked and only Alan Rough, who looked as if he couldn't be bothered running to the spot where the fracas was taking place, escaped unscathed. I'm not proud to say I would have got involved. I would for sure. I couldn't have stood back like the Hibs 'keeper. Instead, I'm positive, I would have put my tuppence worth in.

Happily for me, however, even I couldn't do that from the stand. Instead, I wandered down to a very quiet dressing-room after we had been beaten 2-1. In situations like that, though, it's not the ordering-off that is the talk of the steamy. Instead, it was the fact that we were beaten that irritated the lads. The result was the most important thing and the fact that we had lost two points was, with respect, far more important than losing the manager.

Not surprisingly, we took a real going-over from the Press afterwards but all we could do was accept it and get on with the job. That meant a date with Falkirk and an Ally McCoist goal gave us two important points with me once again relegated to watching the action which is not, frankly, something I enjoy.

My own season started on 16 August with the visit of Dundee United to Ibrox and if nothing else it coincided with a glorious day weather-wise. And, for that matter, we also chose the first hour or so of the game to produce the kind of football we had been building up to. If it had been a boxing match they would have stopped the contest in that time because we were so far ahead of the Tannadice team it was a mis-match. The place was going berserk as 43,995 fans witnessed the kind of football they hadn't seen for years, if at all. But almost as quickly as they were cheering, so they went silent when we squandered a 2-0 lead courtesy of a McCoist double and eventually lost 3-2. You wouldn't have got a bet on the final scoreline at half-time because United hadn't had a kick.

What we got, however, was a kick up our backsides. The gaffer went potty after the match. He couldn't believe we had been so much in command yet lost and nor could we. There were no excuses and, really, no reasons for our collapse. It happened, although I hate to say it, just like that . . ..

Two points from our first three games wasn't quite what we had anticipated and at that point only Ally McCoist had scored any goals for us. It was a shocking start to the season but after the United match we sat down and thought about it. If we had lost playing really badly there might have been a good deal of unease about the situation. But, instead, we had been beaten through carelessness, casualness, call it what you like. That, at least, we could eradicate. We were also comforted by the thought that it was going to be a long, long season.

Our next match saw us at Stenhousemuir on Skol Cup duty and it was memorable only for goals from the manager and I through headers! Now that doesn't happen too often. The only other thing of interest was a fine performance from 'Muir goalkeeper Lindsay Hamilton which was to contribute to his transfer later in the year to Ibrox.

Back on Premier League duty and we were at Douglas Park which, for a variety of reasons, isn't my favourite place. For one, I don't like the pitch and for another, I always get terrible stick being a local lad. For those reasons, if no other, I got a lot of satisfaction from rolling a free kick for Cammy Fraser to rocket a tremendous strike for a goal. We won 2-1.

Things were picking up, then, but we had a failing that was undoubtedly worrying the gaffer. We had a tendency to ease off when we were ahead. Graeme Souness didn't like that. He insisted Liverpool had always kept their foot on the accelerator and finished off the opposition and it was a fair point. Mind you, we couldn't get in front to enable us to ease off in our next game, the Skol Cup tie against East Fife. We didn't play well even though we were never in any danger of losing and in the end we had to rely on penalties to take us through a difficult game.

It possibly wasn't the preparation we wanted for the first Old Firm game of the season but we shouldn't really have worried. The Ibrox fixture against Celtic, televised live on a Sunday, turned out to be a 1-0 rout in our favour. The scoreline was a joke. We were so superior that the solitary Ian Durrant goal was scant reward. Still, the victory over our arch rivals at least made us really start to believe in ourselves and although it took extra time, we romped home in the Skol Cup quarter-final against Dundee next time out. We did likewise in the League game against Motherwell when I managed a goal from all of two feet. I pushed the ball home with my studs.

My problem, if you can call it that, is that all through my career I have been at least as happy making goals for other players as I have scoring them myself. I get tremendous satisfaction from setting them up for the other lads. That's my bread and butter although, don't get me wrong, I also enjoy knocking them in. I like to think I

Nice one, Graeme. The gaffer celebrates a goal against Aberdeen.

have always managed to create my fair share and I know I helped Robert Fleck to some of the six he scored in our next two games against Clydebank and Ilves Tampere in the first round of the UEFA Cup. Both games were won 4-0, with Robert getting a hat-trick each time. It was an astonishing period for the wee striker who was, essentially, only in the team following an injury to big Colin West at Methil. But in fairness, he grabbed his chance — and his chances — brilliantly and he had a fine season.

There was a temporary hiccup at Dens Park when, minus Butcher through suspension, we lost 1-0. So once again our preparation for a big game — the Skol Cup semi-final against Dundee United — wasn't ideal, but we bounced back with one of our best performances of the season and beat them 2-1. The

159

manager was outstanding and controlled the game from start to finish, aided and abetted by Ted McMinn. It's hard to think of two more contrasting players but both were highly effective against the Tannadice team at Hampden.

Not that the gaffer got too excited about it all. He maintained throughout the Skol Cup run and insisted in the dressing-room that night that we had done nothing really. There was no silverware guaranteed and anyway, he said, the League Championship was still the priority. So there wasn't much chance of anyone at Ibrox getting too excited about the club reaching the first domestic final of the season! Graeme certainly enjoyed the game, the performance and the result but I believe he derived more pleasure from our next fixture.

That was against Aberdeen at Ibrox. The Dons were always a bit of a jinx side to us and the newspapers were also full of talk of ill-feeling between the gaffer and Pittodrie boss Alex Ferguson. That's as maybe and whether or not it's confirmation I wouldn't know, but I don't think I've ever seen our leader quite so happy as he was when he scored the opening goal that day. In the end we won comfortably by 2-0 and he seemed very well pleased. Certainly he was 100 per cent happier than he was when we lost 2-0 to Ilves in the second leg of the UEFA Cup tie a few days later.

It was a nightmare performance and I have to hold up my hands and say that on the night we simply lacked professionalism. It was awful and from my point of view I was taken off and substituted before I was sent off. My opponent baited me all night and I think the bench realised what it might lead to so they did me a favour. But it didn't allow me to escape the manager's wrath along with the rest and it's not something I would want to be on the end of all that often. At least I partially made up for that at Tynecastle next time out and although I was pleased with my goal in the 1-1 draw against Hearts it wasn't quite the goal of the season some pundits described it as.

People often ask me what gets into my head when I go on a run. Well, the answer is simple . . . nothing! I just get by one player and keep on going and the secret of that so-called masterpiece is that I didn't even mean to score! I was looking for someone to give the ball to but instead it got a deflection and went in. So much for my genius.

The goalscoring machine called Cooper did it again in the next game against St Mirren, mind you, but I don't think McCoist and Fleck really had anything to worry about. That needed a late goal

Me in a Euro aerial duel.

to secure the points but we were never in any danger against Hibs when we won 3-0. We weren't under any pressure, either, against Falkirk at Brockville when we won 5-1. But it might surprise a few people to know that I consider that unlikely setting to be the venue for one of the finest 90 minutes I have ever produced. Everything clicked into place for me and I thoroughly enjoyed myself. I set up one goal for Ally with a mazy run and he admitted to me after he tapped it in that he was embarrassed claiming it. Then there was a penalty drama when we got a spot kick which seemed the ideal way for Robert Fleck to complete another of his hat-tricks. I was the regular penalty taker but like the rest of the lads presumed the wee man would take it until, that is, I looked to the stand where the manager was sitting out the action. He was pointing and gesticulating that he wanted me to take it. Now, I didn't want to look the greedy one and take the ball off Robert so I shouted to him to take a glance over to the gaffer and when he saw the signals he didn't waste much time handing me the responsibility. In the end it worked out OK because I scored and he went on to get three goals anyway. It was the manager's way of making a point that victory for the team is more important than personal glory and it was an interesting illustration of the way his mind works.

Our next match was the UEFA Cup game against Boavista at Ibrox and although we won 2-1 we didn't play particularly well. I think we perhaps thought they were better than they actually were. But we knew exactly what our next opponents were all about because it was Celtic in the Skol Cup Final at Hampden.

We went down to Troon to prepare for the big day and that gave me the opportunity to do something I had been meaning to do for ages. For years I have been receiving lovely letters from a dear old lady called Isa Anderson who has obviously been following my career closely since day one. She lives in Troon but I had never found the ideal opportunity to meet her until then. I jumped in a taxi at our hotel, gave the driver the address and when she answered the door the look on her face was something I'll never forget. I don't think she could really believe it but it gave me a tremendous feeling to know I had helped make her day and she reminds me of the incident when she writes now.

The final itself wasn't a great sporting occasion. But then again, they seldom are. It was too tense to be very good and I suppose the highlight, although it didn't seem so at the time, was Brian McClair's equaliser after Ian Durrant had put us ahead. It was a smashing strike from the Celt but happily it didn't mean a lot

Glasgow Rangers are smiles better as we celebrate a Skol Cup victory over Celtic.

because I scored the winner from the penalty spot after Roy Aitken downed Terry Butcher. I can honestly say I have never been more confident taking a spot kick and there was never any danger of me missing it. All the madness that went on around us thereafter was irrelevant to Rangers. We had won the Cup and that was all that mattered.

Once more, though, the manager didn't exactly burst blood vessels in his excitement and made it clear the Skol Cup was simply a stepping-stone to greater things. Just seconds after the final whistle he was reminding us again that the title was the priority.

It was too hectic to dwell on that success anyway and two draws against Dundee United and Celtic followed before we achieved an excellent 1-0 win over Boavista in Portugal thanks principally to a wonder save from Chris Woods and the goal from Derek Ferguson.

Our first defeat for a while came at the hands of Motherwell and I can't believe their tactics that day were good for football. They allowed us to camp in their half yet sneaked away and won the game by a single goal. I suppose you have to make do with what you've got but it appalls me nevertheless.

Clydebank and Dundee were despatched when we got back on the rails but a dreadful Cammy Fraser mistake and the ordering-off

163

of Dave McPherson meant the loss of a further two points against Aberdeen at Pittodrie before we were back in Euro action. The tie against Borussia Moenchengladbach was, basically, lost at Ibrox when a silly goal conceded meant we could only draw 1-1. It was all the more frustrating because it was to be the last goal we gave away for weeks — yet such a crucial one. There was no way Hearts, St Mirren and Hibs could beat Chris Woods before we took on the Germans again on their own patch and Borussia couldn't do it either. Unfortunately, we didn't score ourselves so we were out on the away goals rule.

I would love to be able to leave that aspect of this tale there but I can't. It wasn't a good night for me. I was hacked down every time I got the ball and never seemed to be able to make much progress without being impeded one way or the other. It was a frustrating night and I got booked in the first half by Belgian referee Alexis Ponnet. We thought we might have had a penalty at one point but an inglorious night was capped by both Stuart Munro and I being ordered off.

I have to say I thought we were a bit unfortunate but the referee makes the decisions he feels are right and in fairness he has to do that in an instance. It was all a bit of a disaster for us, though, and for myself particularly when he appeared to show me a yellow card for a second time but that's just not possible, of course, and he very quickly changed yellow to red at a stroke. Later, and after I had been banned for three Euro games as a result, I learned that he said I called him "A dirty German" but that was just not the case. Apart from anything else, I realised that as we were playing in Germany there would hardly be a German referee.

But the orderings-off were not the real disaster of the night. That was reserved for the overall result and Terry Butcher, for one, was crying as he saw his European dream disappearing. The gaffer wasn't too bad because he knew as well as anyone that we had been a little unlucky.

If there was any consolation at all to be gained from taking the Euro exit doors then it was the continuing form of the back four and goalkeeper Chris Woods and their run of "clean sheets" proved what everyone really knew. That a sound defence was the basis for success.

They continued that form through meetings with Falkirk and Hamilton as we built up to games over Christmas and New Year that we knew would be crucial to our Championship aspirations. We realised, too, that we would cut Celtic's lead if we could beat

Eyes down, look in and get out of the way of a flying German boot.

them on New Year's Day and we always reasoned that if we could only catch the Parkhead men and get level with them then there would be no stopping us. I believed fervently that those two games against Dundee United — also challenging in a great race — and our Old Firm rivals would go a long way in determining the eventual outcome and it was clear the public at large reckoned that as well because I've never known tickets to be so in demand for a Glasgow derby in particular as they were then. Our performances, as it turned out, were excellent and we won both games courtesy of McCoist and Fleck each time. Those results must have put the fear of death into the rest of the country and if they didn't then newcomer Graham Roberts certainly would.

"Robbo" was signed from Tottenham and he came at just the right time to give everyone a lift. His reputation, it seemed, preceded him but no one at Ibrox is under any illusions about how important he was. He showed that in some style when, on a night in which the eskimos would have taken cover, he warmed the hearts of our fans with a wonder goal against Motherwell at Fir Park.

The bandwagon rolled on against Clydebank and it really was a pleasure to be playing. There was no let-up, either, against Hamilton at Ibrox although the occasion was soured by the double ordering-off of Roberts and Ian Durrant and I can only express my opinion and say that Graham was particularly unlucky. It meant going into battle against Aberdeen without the pair of them so we weren't too disappointed with a no-score draw even if it was at home. It also meant that Chris Woods had forgotten what it was like to take the ball out of the net except in training where the Scots lads beat him more or less at will! So it was no surprise when he received a standing ovation from the 35,000 crowd when he broke the British record for shut-outs in the first half of our Scottish Cup-tie against Hamilton. It was a magnificent achievement — well over 1,000 minutes unbeaten — and thoroughly deserved.

Like the rest of us, though, he would gladly have forfeited that if he had known what was just around the corner. Football has a habit of kicking you up the backside just as you think you are going well and that's one reason why I have never counted chickens in my time. But even I wasn't prepared for the slip that allowed Adrian Sprott through to score what proved to be the only goal of the game. It was a disaster but what irritated me just as much, or nearly, was the way it was written up afterwards. It was all about wonderful Hamilton despite them being about the most negative team you'll ever see. I've said it before and I'll say it again . . .

Eyes down, perfect balance and style . . . is this me?

167

performances like that can't be good for football.

Not that Accies cared too much and it was pure hell for me being a local lad. People started to come up and talk to me about Hamilton being our bogy team, yet when you looked back at the end of the season they managed to win just one game out of five! The manager, though, put it into perspective when he said: "It is part of Rangers' history now, albeit an unhappy part, but we just have to put it behind us."

That's exactly what we did and we demolished Hearts in a match memorable for breaking their long unbeaten home run and about the worst miss of my career when I somehow sent a close-range header wide of the post! St Mirren were "gubbed" as well and in those two games McCoist and Fleck, singled out for most of the Cup criticism, answered everyone by scoring six goals between them. It was no more than they deserved and I think they enjoyed those strikes more than most.

A friendly against Bordeaux was a pleasant interruption to the more serious action and we won 3-2 without me, which was a bit worrying! It was the only game I missed apart from the opening two in the season. But I was back for a draw against Hibs and a victory over Falkirk at Brockville, then a home win over Hamilton during which I took great delight in having a dig at Adrian Sprott. He was in the Accies' defensive wall as I lined up a free kick and I couldn't resist calling over to him that his name wouldn't be in the newspapers this time. We won 2-0.

By now we were top of the League and going well and I don't think anything would have stopped us from winning the title after that. It was an interesting mix in the team with youngsters like Ian Durrant and the English lads chasing glory for the first time and me going for a second Championship medal, but nine years after the first. There was, as you would expect, tremendous pressure but with lads like McCoist and Jimmy Nicholl in the dressing-room there was bags of laughter as well. These guys are great for taking the strain out of it. Nevertheless, it was all a little nervy as it was bound to be and it was clearly affecting the supporters as much as us. There were times you could have heard a pin drop in an Ibrox filled to capacity. It was remarkable.

Graeme Souness reacted to the pressure by virtually banning us from listening to half-time scores. It is the practice at games for the interval scores to be given from around the country but the gaffer didn't want us hearing or seeing them. He kept telling us that as long as we were winning that was the main thing. If we could do it

Davie Hay sits it out but he and I were both award winners on this occasion unlike later in the year when the likeable Hay parted company with Celtic after Rangers' runaway League success.

in style so much the better, of course, and we did just that against Dundee at Dens Park in the middle of March. It was a vital game — weren't they all? — and I can't recall the lads being psyched up quite as much as before that match. We were brilliant and won 4-0 without giving them a kick. It was a sensational performance and as good as anything we put together all season. We were back on Tayside a few days later, across the road at Tannadice, and we knew Celtic would be looking for us slipping up there. We won 1-0 and that must have been a real sickener for the Parkhead men.

We had a similar victory over Motherwell at Ibrox although I didn't play too much of a part in the action following a nasty shoulder injury. It bothered me again against Celtic and I had to go off to be replaced by Jimmy Phillips. We lost 3-1 and although the result gave Celtic a glimmer of hope it was no more than that and while we were unhappy we weren't sidetracked. You could sense in the dressing-room that we weren't about to let all our good work go for nothing at this stage and Dundee, Clydebank and Hearts went the way of so many others as we regained complete control.

So when we travelled north to our hotel on Friday, 1 May, we knew that the title was within our grasp. To be frank, we didn't necessarily expect to grab the glory at Pittodrie because no one connected with Rangers would have presumed to be champions. Had we been beaten and Celtic won it would have meant going into the last Saturday of the season with us two points ahead of our old rivals and with a superior goal difference. It needed to be mathematically impossible for them to catch us and it wouldn't have been if the above scenario had come to pass.

That's why the champagne was conspicious by its absence although the fans who milled around the hotel in Aberdeen didn't seem to share our caution. They were everywhere and it was impossible to contemplate letting them down. We didn't and we got the draw we needed — minus the manager, who was sent off — and even the point was irrelevant when we heard that Falkirk had astonishingly beaten Celtic at Parkhead.

The final whistle sparked some of the most amazing scenes I have been involved with as thousands of Rangers fans who had been locked out were allowed in to celebrate. The pitch was swamped with supporters and for a while it was quite frightening as the players struggled to get to the dressing-room. I got a whack in the face but I'm fairly confident it was unintentional! In the end, it took a couple of Grampian's finest to rescue me and take me to safety where Graeme Souness was waiting to greet and congratulate all the lads individually.

It goes almost without saying that it was a fantastic feeling, maybe even better than my first time what seemed like a century before. I went back home with a mate and we had a celebration meal with family and friends. It's fair to say it was a good night. It's even fairer to say it was a brilliant night.

It left us knowing that our final game of the season against St Mirren, which might have been a tricky little fixture had things worked out differently, was going to be party time. The week building up to that match and following the title victory was great. You couldn't move for folk adding their congratulations and it was a very sweet feeling. In due course, Saints came and lost 1-0 and while they did well they must have felt like gatecrashers. Our fans came dressed as Teddy Bears, there was a Santa Claus and generally it was an afternoon everyone enjoyed to the full.

It brought to an end a stunningly successful season for Rangers and I would hope I played my part in it all. Certainly, I enjoyed almost every minute of it and it made up in no small way for the years of nothing I had played through at Ibrox.

The season had not been without its disasters and while Hamilton and Borussia will rank high among them I was desperately sorry for the likes of Bobby Russell, Colin West and Cammy Fraser who all spent a long time injured and the latter, indeed, had to retire. I was sorry, too, to see Ted McMinn go because I enjoyed his antics and he is a lovely lad.

But the good far outweighed the bad and if there was a single reason for our success it was Graeme Souness. The manager changed things in a revolutionary way. There were the well-documented regulations about no golf and the use of flip-flops in the stadium and it was the wee things like that that somehow made the whole set-up more professional. I don't want to go overboard because I'll only get stick but he is a remarkable man and manager. The season gave him enormous pleasure and after the success, in an identical role, of his great pal Kenny Dalglish at Liverpool he was clearly thrilled. He has also been the first to pay tribute to the significant impact Walter Smith has had on events. Wattie proved the ideal foil to the gaffer and although he simply can't play the game he definitely knows a bit about it!

On the playing side everyone made a contribution. But perhaps Terry Butcher stood out from the others. He's a Man Mountain and his presence at the back helped us tighten up considerably in a key area. He's also such an enthusiast and a born winner that it's difficult to come to terms with the fact that he's English. Still, maybe he'll get over that.

171

But while season 1986-87 was phenomenal for Rangers it is, as Graeme Souness likes to say, history now and while he allowed himself a few days of celebration after our success his thoughts quickly turned to the future.

During the summer, in fact, he sold Dave McPherson and Hugh Burns to Hearts and recruited John McGregor from Liverpool, Avi Cohen eventually from Israel, Mark Falco from Watford and Trevor Francis from Atalanta. Nothing stands still at Ibrox.

So where to Rangers and Davie Cooper go from here . . . ?

The end of a long, hard season. But this is the moment we all worked towards as the champagne flows and the League Championship Trophy is safely in Terry Butcher's hands.

Chapter Fourteen

PLANNING AHEAD

RANGERS, with last year's successes behind us, will now go from strength to strength. It was Graeme Souness who said the title triumph and the Skol Cup was just the beginning and I can see all his dreams becoming reality. The European Cup is obviously the big one and while his number one target will be the League Championship every season there's no doubt winning in Europe is vitally important. He did it as a player and he's never disguised the fact that he is desperately keen to do it as a manager.

Is he being over-ambitious? I don't think so. Rangers are now geared to compete, in every sense, with the best in Europe and we might even have won the UEFA Cup last season but for certain circumstances. We have progressed since then, though, and with the players we now have at Ibrox I see no reason why the European Cup should be a pipedream. Rangers have the kind of defensive strength that is so important in two-leg ties and that would give anyone a base for confidence. Terry Butcher, Chris Woods, Graham Roberts, Jimmy Nicholl and the others have all been over the course before and know how these matches are played. And, equally important, we have the quality players elsewhere who can create and score goals in any setting. Put it together and in my mind's eye I can see the European Cup would fit nicely into our magnificent Trophy Room at the stadium.

In more general terms, Rangers will continue to improve under Graeme Souness and Walter Smith. It's obvious the two have formed an excellent partnership and I cannot imagine Rangers ever sacking them. The way things are going that seems unthinkable. On the other hand, maybe the time will come when Graeme and Walter lose a bit of their enthusiasm and will seek a new challenge together or separately. The manager throughout his career has wanted to do new, exciting things with his life. Going to Sampdoria was a classic example of that because he could have stayed at Liverpool quietly and efficiently going about his business. Instead he opted for a change of country, not just a change of club, because it represented an exciting new challenge at just the right time. It was the same story when he came back from Italy to Ibrox. He wouldn't have been short of offers to go to lesser clubs yet he jumped in at the deep end with, as we know now, a fair measure of success.

He's still playing, too, although I wouldn't expect him to continue that side of his career for too much longer. Certainly not in this day and age, which brings me to a point I need to raise before I finish. I watch the occasional game from years ago on the television and I admire the skills and talents of the players from bygone days. But I have to say I don't believe they could survive in modern-day football. It annoys me when people compare current players with guys from decades ago and say we couldn't lace their boots. On the contrary, I don't think they would find it at all easy nowadays. The pace of the game is so much quicker and you can't beat one opponent and then make directly for goal like you used to be able to. Now, you're likely to find a queue of players waiting for you. It is, literally, a whole new ball game. I'm only sticking up for this generation generally and before anyone starts knocking me, I can assure you I have tremendous respect for the players of 20 years ago for what they did then.

But, enough. I am beginning to think of other things. Like my own career. I feel a little bit frustrated that these good and exciting times at Ibrox have come a little too late for me. I can see success following success and I would have liked to be part of that for the years to come. But against that frustration is the realism that I have enjoyed — cancel that, am still enjoying — a marvellous career that others would give their right arms for, so I can't be greedy. Instead, I simply want to take advantage of the time left for me and enjoy it.

I have been promised a testimonial by Rangers and hopefully I

The family at home . . . Christine, Blue and I.

will be able to continue playing for this season and next . . . for Rangers. Right now there's no way I would play for anyone else. I just can't imagine wearing a different strip.

175

I will know better than anyone when the time comes for me to pack it up and when that happens I will make a clean break from the game. I don't intend to let myself go into the reserves at Ibrox or drift down the leagues to let lesser players line up and have a kick at Davie Cooper. When I finish I want to be a Rangers first-team player. What we're talking about here, of course, is an ideal world and all my current thoughts are based on being reasonably financially secure. A testimonial, hopefully, will help in that direction and then I can retire in a couple of years without too much worry. I don't have any desire to be particularly wealthy, and never have done. As long as Christine and I are comfortable then that's good enough. Obviously I'm lucky in that that could work out but I've never taken anything for granted and I wouldn't start now.

I can only outline my "masterplan" and hope that's how things pan out. No one knows what's around the corner. If it does work out the way I hope then my break from football will be complete. I hardly envisage myself as manager or coach. How could I when I have hated training all these years? I don't have the patience, anyway. Instead, I would think about having a business. I have always fancied the thought of a small restaurant where Christine and I could look after the people personally. We're both quite keen on the idea.

We have no particular plans to have children but in case anyone puts too much emphasis on what the gutter press claimed at one stage last year we're as happy together now as we were when we got married. We're thinking together about what the future holds for the Coopers. But, equally, we're not spending every waking minute wondering about what I will do when I finish playing.

Right now I'm with Rangers and hopefully I will be for a while to come. Once a Bluenose always a Bluenose. Or did someone say True Blue?